Baby Boomer's Guide to Estate & Medicaid Planning

Baby Boomer's Guide to Estate & Medicaid Planning

Planning for Yourself and Your Parents

Jon A. Iverson, JD

Stonemark Publishing Co.

Baby Boomer's Guide to Estate & Medicaid Planning
Copyright © 2005 by Jon A. Iverson
All rights reserved

Cover and book design: Patricia Broersma
Illustrations: Don Thomas

ISBN 0-9657936-2-1

Library of Congress Control No.
2005904541

Printed in the United States of America

STONEMARK PUBLISHING COMPANY
P.O. Box 687
Medford, OR 97501

ACKNOWLEDGEMENTS

The author is grateful to the attorneys who contributed their superior
knowledge and critiqued some of the more specialized topics:

Victoria E. Blair
Fleming & Curti, PLC
Tucson, Arizona

Cinda Conroyd
Douglas & Conroyd PC
Salem, Oregon

Melanie E. Marmion
Fitzwater & Meyer LLP
Clackamas, Oregon

CONTENTS

EXAMPLES

INTRODUCTION

Baby Boomer's Guide is not a "do-it-yourself" manual, but a concise, refreshingly readable survey of essential topics. A special section is devoted to Medicaid and its role in long-term care strategies. The book is written to help people work more knowledgeably, efficiently and confidently with legal and financial professionals.

Already more than 22 million American households are caring for an aging relative, and the number of Americans 65 and over is expected to double over the next 25 years. This book is intended to give perspective on the aging issues with which many of us will be confronted. Whether concerned about the problems associated with incapacity or about the transfer of assets after death, the reader will should find a great deal of help in the pages that follow.

Part I - Wills and Probate is the beginning point in deciding upon an estate plan. One needs to understand what a will can and cannot accomplish in order to make informed decisions about an estate plan. Some assets are governed by a deceased person's will and some are not, depending on the type of asset and how titled. Assets subject to a will must be "probated" (except for the very smallest of estates). In addition, Part I (and Appendix B) will be an asset for someone who has been nominated as executor of someone's will - it will give good insight into the probate process and what his or her responsibilities as executor will be.

Methods of avoiding probate are discussed in **Part II - Avoiding Probate**. The manner in which an asset is titled (and the beneficiary designations) will determine whether or not title will pass to the successor owner without probate after the owner's death. Joint tenancy is probably the most common way of avoiding probate; Chapter 3 should be read for a clear explanation of the risks and limitations of joint tenancy. Chapter 4 explains fixed and variable annuities and their shortcomings as investment vehicles.

Part III is devoted to **Living Trusts**. Living trusts are a popular way to avoid probate, particularly in states with high probate costs. They can also serve to avoid the need for a guardianship or conservatorship to manage income and assets in the event of incapacity. Chapter 8 will help you decide between a trust and a will, and Chapter 9 explains the duty of the trustee of a trust (and executor of an estate) to file a fiduciary tax return.

Part IV - Taxable Estates explains the operation of the federal gift-estate tax law. If your estate would exceed the exemption amount, go to Chapter 10 for an explanation of how the unified gift-estate tax works. Chapter 11 highlights the income tax benefits and estate tax benefits of charitable giving.

Part V covers **Health Care and Health Care Finance**. Chapter 12 is devoted to living wills and health care powers of attorney. It is usually advisable to appoint an agent under a health care power of attorney, even if you have a living will.

If you are considering the purchase of a long-term care insurance policy, don't miss Chapter 13. It explains the choices to be made in purchasing a policy and illustrates the devastating effect inflation can have on your coverage.

If you (or your parents) have limited income and assets and would be candidates for Medicaid assistance in the event long-term care became necessary, then you will be vitally interested in Chapter 14. A substantial portion of the book is devoted to this complicated topic because it has so many different aspects.

Lastly, if you serve as executor of a will, trustee of a trust, agent under a power of attorney, guardian, or conservator, you are a "fiduciary" in the eyes of the law and subject to certain legal responsibilities of which you should be aware. The detailed **Appendices** in this book will help you understand those responsibilities.

– Jon A. Iverson, J.D.

PART I

Wills & Probate

CHAPTER ONE

WILLS

Wills are such a basic part of estate planning that everyone should be familiar with their uses and the probate process in general. A well-conceived estate plan will almost always include a will, even if it is intended only as a backup or complement to some other vehicle, such as a trust.

Very simply, a will is the written statement of a person's wishes as to the disposition of his or her property after death. It does not take effect until death and applies to the situation as it exists at the time of death. Since it does not take effect until death, it can be amended or revoked at any time, as long as the person retains the mental capacity to do a will. The person executing the will is known as the "testator" in the case of men and "testatrix" in the case of women. In most states, the signature of the testator or testatrix must be witnessed by two competent witnesses.

The witnesses should be in the physical presence of the person signing the will, see him or her sign, and then sign in response to the testator's request that they sign as witnesses.

A surprising number of people believe that without a will, their estates will pass to the state. Although that could happen if you only had distant relatives, the overwhelming majority of people have siblings, nieces, nephews, aunts, uncles, cousins, or descendants of cousins who would be heirs at law in the absence of a will.

With surprising regularity, I also encounter people who think that by having a will, a probate will be avoided! This is definitely not the case, as it depends on what assets are owned and how they are titled – a probate proceeding may or may not be needed. This subject is covered in Chapters 2 and 8 and in Appendix B.

WHAT A WILL ACCOMPLISHES.

Avoids intestacy. You need a will to avoid intestacy! A person who dies with a valid will in effect is said to have died "testate," while someone who dies without a will dies "intestate." The laws of intestacy, governing who inherits a deceased person's estate in the absence of a will, are also known as the laws of "descent and distribution." To best understand the benefits of a will, you need an understanding of the laws of intestacy.

In the case of intestacy, state law will dictate who inherits your probate assets. The laws of intestacy differ somewhat from one state to the next. But, in general, if the deceased person had no children, his or her entire estate typically passes to the surviving spouse. If the decedent had children, part might pass to the children and part to the surviving spouse. Again, this varies since each state legislature has made its own assumption as to what the decedent would have wanted. In some states, the entire estate passes to the surviving spouse if all the decedent's children were born of that marriage; i.e., the where decedent had no children from a prior marriage. If there is no surviving spouse, the entire estate typically goes to the decedent's children. If there are no children or spouse, to the parents, siblings, then to grandparents, aunts and uncles, nieces and nephews, cousins, etc. If there is no surviving grandparent or descendant of grandparents (aunts, uncles, cousins), the estate might go to the state; i.e., in many states you cannot go higher up the family tree than grandparents in the search of living heirs. That is, you can trace up to grandparents (both sides) and then down to descendants of the grandparents. But if there were no descendants of grandparents, you could not go up to great grandparents and start tracing down.

The laws of intestacy are rigid. They give no consideration to the circumstances or needs of the individual heirs. Although the results of intestacy might approximate the wishes of someone who is survived by a spouse or children, that would seldom be true in the case of more distant relatives.

Allows special bequests. Even if you would want the bulk of your estate to go to your spouse, children, or other heirs at law under the intestacy laws of your state, you might not want them to get every last item. You might want your golf clubs to go to your golf partner, for instance. Or, you might want to leave a bequest to your church or favorite charity. If you do not have a will setting forth such wishes, your heirs at law would take all. If you wanted to give your car to someone in particular, a will would also allow you to direct that any loan be paid by the estate.

Avoids right of representation. Even if the intestacy laws of your state would give your estate to the desired people, there can be other good reasons for having a will. Let's assume that you are not married. Your children will divide your estate equally under the intestacy laws of your state and that would be fine with you. But what if one of your children predeceases you? Intestacy laws usually give the estate to the heirs "by right of representation," meaning that if one child were to predecease you, his or her children (your grandchildren) would divide the deceased child's share equally. For example, assume you had two children, one of whom died before you. Your deceased child was survived by your two grandchildren, both of whom have drug or alcohol problems or whom you regard as spendthrifts. If you would want your surviving child to take everything, to the exclusion of the two irresponsible grandchildren, a will would be needed. Otherwise, the two grandchildren would divide one half and be free to spend it as they chose.

Handles unequal loans to children. Another fairly common scenario is where one child has borrowed money but the other child or children have not. If one child has been favored with significant loans or advances, most state intestacy laws require the loan to be treated as an advance; i.e., offset against the indebted child's share of the inheritance. If you would want the inequality handled differently after your death, those wishes should be clearly set forth in a will. As a practical matter, of course, there should always be a promissory note from the indebted child and a record of payments to avoid a potential dispute as to the state of affairs.

Nominates a guardian for minor children. In addition to allowing a person to specify which relative, friend or charity is to get what portion of one's estate, a will is the proper vehicle for nominating a guardian for minor children. The surviving spouse as the natural parent would, of course, be next in line as custodian. But what if the other parent is also deceased? What if both spouses die in the same accident? What if the parents are divorced and the surviving non-custodial would decline the responsibility?

Parents with minor children should give thought to these possibilities, however remote they may seem, and explore with potential guardians their willingness to assume the awesome responsibility of raising their children. A will is the place to nominate a guardian for your minor children, as well as setting forth the terms of any children's trust into which you would want your estate to be distributed.

Appoints an executor. One of the most important reasons to have a will is that it allows you to nominate an executor, executrix, or personal representative of your own choosing. (These synonyms all refer to the court-appointed fiduciary who administers the estate. For the sake of simplicity and without regard to gender, they are usually referred to in this book as "executor.")

If you died without a will (or failed to nominate one in your will), state law would determine who is to serve. The order of preference is likely to be somewhat like this, with the state department of revenue near the bottom:

- **Person nominated in the will, if any**

- **Surviving spouse**

- **Children**

- **Creditor**

The executor is a fiduciary whose responsibility it is to take care of the administration of the estate — identify and gather the assets of the estate, pay creditors and taxing authorities, and distribute what remains in accordance with the terms of the will. An executor has considerable power and can exercise discretion in ways that could affect the other beneficiaries as well as creditors. It is the executor, for instance, who decides what fair market values should be assigned to the various assets. The executor normally decides who gets which items of personal property in the event of a disagreement. It is important that someone be nominated who is will be fair and impartial, particularly if sibling rivalry exists.

The choice of executor is particularly important where there are step-children. Blood relationship — or, more accurately, the lack thereof — is a pre-existing battle line which makes the prospect of litigation more than a remote possibility. A good deal of the case law on wills and intestacy (as well as trusts) has been made in litigation between the surviving spouse and his or her stepchildren. If the right executor is named in the will, the chance of litigation will have been lessened. Even if the decedent and surviving spouse entered into a pre-nuptial agreement before their second marriage disclaiming all interest in each other's estate, the selection of the executor can help calm a situation where hard feelings come easily.

People who sense a potential dispute upon their demise sometimes think in terms of naming one person from each camp and hope they will work out any differences. It would be better to name an independent third party to act as executor, even if it ends up costing the estate more money. Anything that avoids litigation will be an investment with great returns!

Note that the possibility of a dispute will not necessarily be diminished by using a trust rather than a will. A dissatisfied beneficiary inclined to litigate can always find some reason to initiate litigation. The grounds for challenging trusts are almost the same as in a will contest – undue influence, incapacity of the trustor, overreaching, and the like. The successor trustee of a revocable living trust should be selected with the same forethought as an executor because the successor trustee performs essentially the same role as an executor. But without court supervision.

Avoids the cost of a bond. If someone dies without a will and an intestate probate proceeding is required, the court will almost always require a probate bond to protect the creditors and heirs at law against misappropriation by the executor. The executor will have access to all the income and assets in the probate estate and could go on a spending spree or take a trip to Las Vegas. In recognition of this risk, state probate codes require a probate bond to protect interested parties against misappropriation of estate funds. However, the cost of the bond can be avoided by doing a will and waiving the bond requirement right in the will. Courts will usually honor such a waiver. If you fully trust the person named in your will to serve as executor (which should always be the case), then it makes sense to waive the bond requirement. Do so right in the will.

WHAT A WILL CANNOT ACCOMPLISH.

There are several things, however, that a will cannot accomplish. As a general rule, you can leave your estate to whomever you wish. Except in Louisiana, you can disinherit your children or favor one child over anoth-

In most cases, family will be the natural object of a person's bounty. However, a caregiver might make the grade.

er. However, you cannot completely disinherit your spouse. If a deceased person omitted his or her spouse from the will, the surviving spouse can elect to take a portion of the estate, despite the terms of the will. This right has traditionally been known as "dower and curtesy," but it has been codified by statute and is now commonly referred to as a "forced" share or "elective" share. Under these statutes the surviving spouse is given the right to elect against the will and to take some minimum percentage or amount, as established by the state legislature. The forced share laws vary widely from one state to the next, so few generalizations can be made. For example, in some states the forced share amount can be taken out of only the probate estate; i.e., those assets that are subject to probate administration and listed in the inventory. In those states, non-probate assets (jointly-owned assets, retirement accounts, annuities, living trusts, etc.) escape the elective share. If the decedent had placed all of his or her assets in a living trust, the surviving spouse could be completely disinherited.

In other states, the surviving spouse is also entitled to a percentage of the decedent's augmented estate, such as joint accounts, IRAs, living trusts and other non-probate assets. And there are other variations, such as a maximum percentage or total that the surviving spouse can acquire by electing against the will. The forced share amount may be offset by other assets which the surviving spouse acquires by reason of the death, such as life insurance, annuities and jointly-owned property.

Interestingly, the right to elect against the deceased's spouse's will does not exist in community property states (California, New Mexico, Louisiana, Nevada, Texas, Washington, Idaho, Arizona, and Wisconsin). There is no conceptual need for it under a community property system because the surviving spouse, by definition, already owns half of all community property, regardless of how it was titled. In a community property system, a person has the power to dispose by will of all his or her separate property but only half of the community property. The other half of the community property belongs to the surviving spouse.

Community property consists of everything acquired during the existence of the marital community (i.e., while married and living in a community property state) except that which is acquired by gift or inheritance. The initial issue is not whose name is on the account but when it was acquired. If an item was acquired during marriage, it will be presumed to be community property, even if titled solely in the decedent's name. However, if the deceased spouse's beneficiaries can prove that an asset in the decedent's name was acquired by gift or inheritance or purchased with the decedent's separate funds, then it would separate property, even though it was acquired during marriage. Absent such proof, an asset acquired during marriage would be classified as community property and belong half to the surviving spouse. If an item was acquired before marriage and has not been re-titled or commingled with other assets, it is separate property. Each community property state has a series of presumptions for categorizing an asset as community or separate and differing ways of resolving issues of commingling and appreciation in value.

REQUISITES OF A VALID WILL.

There are numerous requirements of a will, and the discussion below covers only the shortcomings that commonly arise in will contests.

Mental Competency. The testator or testatrix must be mentally competent at the time he or she signs the will. When wills are challenged, the challenge will invariably include allegations that the testator was not competent when the will was signed. These allegations are usually accompanied by claims that the person favored by the will exercised undue influence to get the will signed. The weaker the testator was at the time and the more "unnatural" the disposition, the easier it will be to convince the judge or jury of undue influence or lack of mental capacity.

In general, to be mentally competent, one must know:

- **Who the natural objects of his or her bounty are.** In most cases, spouses and children will be the natural objects of a person's bounty. A care giver of several years might make the grade, but one who had looked after the decedent during the last month of his or her life would have an uphill battle in convincing a judge or jury that the decedent was competent and had not been unduly influenced.

- **The nature and extent of his or her estate.** Did the testator know what he or she owned and the value?

The fact that the health of the testator had failed before the will was signed does not necessarily equate to a lack of competence. The question always remains: did the person know the objects of his or her bounty, and did the person know what he or she owned *at the time the will was signed?* Most elderly people have good days and bad days as their health fails. As long as the two-pronged test was met at the time of signing (and it can be proved later), the will should be upheld. Obviously, the facts and circumstances become all important if competency will be an issue, so great care should be taken to document the circumstances and mental state of the person at the time of signing.

Note also that it is not necessary that a mentally competent testator or testatrix be physically able to sign – someone else can make a mark at his or her direction in lieu of an actual signature. Or, the signer can make his or her own mark. Again, the weaker the person, the easier it would be as a practical matter to challenge his or her competency. But the two-pronged test still applies.

Clear disposition of property. Wills normally give instructions to pay debts and expenses of last illness and then state who gets what. (Debts would be paid first even if the will was silent on the matter). After bequests of specific items of property and gifts of money, the will should dispose of the remainder – i.e., "I give the rest of my estate to my children by right of representation." The last four words, as well as *"per stirpes,"* simply mean that if one child dies, his or her children will divide the deceased child's share. If the will said *"per capita,"* then the surviving children would each take a larger share to the exclusion of descendants of the deceased child. It is important that the instructions be clear. I recall one case where the deceased parent, I was convinced, intended to leave his entire estate to his disabled son who had lived with him. He got a will form from the stationery store, filled it out and had it witnessed at the bank. The problem was that although he listed all of his assets, he failed to state that "I give my estate to XXX." Without words of disposition, the trial court was unable to agree with the disabled son that the testamentary intent was to leave it all to him. The estate was divided pursuant to the laws of intestacy, as though the "will" had never been written.

Witnessing requirements. In general, any person of sound mind over the age of 18 can make a will. However, most states require that it be in writing and require two witnesses to the signing. Both witnesses should be in the room at the same time and see the testator or testatrix sign the will. The person signing the will should request them to sign as witnesses.

Some states, however, recognize unwitnessed wills written in the decedent's own handwriting, known as "holographic" wills. If a holographic will is valid in the state where it was executed, it will be recognized in another state where probate is being sought, even if that state does not recognize holographic wills.

EXAMPLE 1.

Will must be valid where executed. Bill wrote an un-witnessed will in his own hand while living in State A, which recognizes holographic wills. He later moved to State B to be near his daughter. He died in State B and a probate was necessary. State B admitted the will to probate because it was proved to be valid in State A.

In order to get a will admitted to probate, it must be established to the court's satisfaction that the witnessing formalities were complied with and that the testator or testatrix was of sound legal mind. This is ordinarily done by affidavit of the witnesses. In order to avoid having to locate the witnesses years later after the person the will was signed, the current practice in most locales is to have the witnesses sign an affidavit attached to the will at the same time they witness the testator's signing. Such a will is said to be "self-executing" or "self-proving."

A will can also be proved formally by taking the testimony of the witnesses. This is not normally done unless there is a will contest.

TITLING OF ASSETS.

Let's assume that a family member passed away having a will in place. Or that he or she did not have a will, so that the law of intestacy will dictate who inherits. Either way, there is one additional and *very critical* consideration to keep in mind. That has to do with how the deceased person's assets were titled. Whose name is on the account? What is the form of ownership? Many people fail to understand the extreme importance of titling of their assets. The most carefully conceived estate plan can be rendered meaningless if the assets are owned in the wrong name or wrong type of ownership.

Certain forms of asset ownership are covered by a will (or intestacy); others are not. *It is the type of ownership that determines whether or not succession of ownership is even governed by the will (or intestacy).* After death, each of the decedent's assets must be examined to determine the type of ownership. If an asset is owned in one of the following forms, succession of ownership will *not* be governed by either the will or by the laws of intestacy – title will pass directly to the surviving co-owners by operation of law or pursuant to a beneficiary designation:

- **Tenancy by entireties** (real property owned as husband and wife - not all states)

- **Joint ownership with right of survivorship**

- **Assets in revocable living trusts**

- **Pay-on-death accounts, Totten trusts, and "in trust for" accounts with banks**

- **Transfer-on-death accounts with brokerage firms**

- **Titled assets disposable by recorded beneficiary deeds** (not all states)

- **Annuities with named beneficiaries**

- **Life insurance with named beneficiaries**

- **Certificates of deposit with named beneficiaries**

- **Individual retirement accounts, 401Ks, 403(b)s, etc. with named beneficiaries**

These various forms of ownership are discussed in detail in Chapters 3, 4 and 5.

A will (and intestacy) controls the disposition of only what I refer to as "probate assets;" that is, assets not owned in one of the above forms of ownership. "Probate assets" include everything else and will consist principally of the following:

- **Assets owned solely in the decedent's name**

- **Assets which are co-owned as tenants in common with others**

The probate process is discussed in detail in the next chapter.

CHAPTER TWO

PROBATE ADMINISTRATION

Everyone has heard of "probate." It is a dread word, about which there is a great deal of misunderstanding. This chapter is intended to clear up the common misunderstandings and give the reader a sense of what is involved in probate administration.

If you pass away owning probate assets, as defined on pages 15 and 16, a probate proceeding will probably be necessary in order to transfer title to your successors. Probate is the court-supervised process in which the court appoints an executor, admits the will to probate (if there was a will) and oversees the administration of the estate. It begins with the filing of a petition with the court to appoint an executor and open the probate proceeding.

The procedure is essentially the same in the case of intestacy, except that because there is no will, the petition asks to have final distribution made to the heirs at law rather than the beneficiaries under the will. If there is not a will with a provision waiving the bond requirement, a probate bond will normally be required by the court. A probate bond is an agreement by an insurance company to protect the estate (up to the amount specified in the bond, of course) in case the executor absconds with estate assets.

Probate assets consist of assets owned solely in the decedent's name and assets which the decedent co-owned with others. A probate proceeding will likely be needed as to such assets. Here are some examples to help clarify when a probate proceeding will be necessary and when it might not. Obviously, it will depend on the probate code of the state in question.

EXAMPLE 2.

Probate assets exceeding the limit - Harry passed away owning a home worth $100,000 in his own name and a bank account. The maximum amount in his state for using a small estate affidavit is $50,000. His heirs or beneficiaries will have no choice but to commence a probate proceeding. The bank will not release funds and the title company will not insure title unless and until they know that the person signing the deed has the authority to do so. That authority emanates from appointment of an executor by the probate court.

EXAMPLE 3.

Tenancy in common - Harry passed away co-owning a vacation home worth $150,000 with his son. The ceiling in his state for the small estate affidavit is $50,000. Since the property is owned as tenants in common and the value of Harry's one-half interest exceeds the small estate limit, a probate proceeding will be necessary. If Harry had owned it with his son as joint tenants with right of survivorship, of course, his son would become the sole owner and probate would not be necessary.

EXAMPLE 4.

Tenancy by the entireties - Harry passed away co-owning real property with his wife as tenants by the entireties. His wife becomes the new owner by operation of law. She will not have to do a probate as to that asset, regardless of the value. The home would not be subject to expenses of last illness or other debts of the decedent.

EXAMPLE 5.

Assets not involving third parties - Harry passed away owning only some antique furniture and a coin collection worth $30,000. He is not married and has only one child, who inherits everything under the laws of intestacy. Despite the fact that the limit for small estate affidavits in Harry's state is only $10,000, a probate might not be needed. That's because there is no certificate of title with respect to either the furniture or the coin collection. The heir can simply take possession of the personal property. However, if the child wanted to sell the collection and a coin dealer asked to see some proof of ownership, there could conceivably be a problem. Of course, creditors always have to be paid.

ROLE OF THE EXECUTOR.

An executor is a court-appointed fiduciary who is responsible for administering the estate. After appointment by the court, the executor is responsible for publishing notice to creditors; giving notice to any other beneficiaries and heirs at law; identifying and taking control of assets of the estate; taking an inventory of and valuing the assets; sometimes liquidating estate assets; paying creditors and taxing authorities; filing the final tax returns; and ultimately distributing what remains to the beneficiaries named in the will or heirs at law, as the case may be. The executor normally hires an attorney to represent him or her in the process, but representation is not mandatory. The executor's responsibilities are discussed further in Appendix B.

After the creditor claim period has expired and the final tax returns have been filed and creditors paid, the executor renders a final accounting. This is a report which accounts for all assets and income that have come into his or her possession and all expenditures that have been made. The accounting, along with a notice of right to object, is mailed to the heirs or beneficiaries and filed with the court. It is incumbent upon the heirs or beneficiaries to object to any irregularities. Otherwise, at the end of the notice period, the court will enter an order which approves the accounting and orders distribution as requested.

After the distribution order has been signed, the assets are distributed. Each heir or beneficiary will sign a receipt to be filed with the court indicating that proper distribution was made. After the receipts have been filed indicating that the estate was properly distributed, the court enters the final order, which discharges the executor, releases the insurance company from further liability on the probate bond, and closes the estate. The process of administering a simple estate from commencement of probate to close could take less than six months in states with a short creditor claim period (assuming the estate was handled expeditiously) to several years for large estates having complex issues.

The process described above is the traditional, formal procedure for a probate. It should be noted that the degree of formality required will vary greatly from one state to the next. Some states have dispensed with almost all formality and allow the executor to administer the estate without court supervision – as long as no one objects. New Jersey, for instance, probably has the most simplified probate procedure. Numerous states have a streamlined probate procedure whereby the court's oversight is suspended after the executor establishes by affidavit that the estate is solvent; i.e., that the estate's assets exceed its liabilities. Beneficiaries, heirs at law, and creditors are entitled to notice, and a petition for relief can be filed if the executor is not handling his or her responsibilities properly. Living trusts are not commonly used as a probate avoidance device in states with streamlined procedures and low probate costs.

A probate bond protects the estate in the case of an executor absconding with the estate assets.

PART II

....

Avoiding Probate

CHAPTER THREE

AVOIDING PROBATE VIA JOINT TENANCY

As discussed in the preceding chapter, only assets owned solely in the decedent's name and assets owned as a tenant in common with others will be governed by the will or by the laws of intestacy. This chapter discusses one very prevalent type of ownership that avoids the need for a court-supervised probate proceeding; namely, joint ownership with right of survivorship. The topic merits an entire chapter because it is not as simple as one might assume.

Joint tenancy could be either desirable or undesirable, depending on the circumstances and objectives. It is important to fully understand the implications of joint ownership and to be sure that joint ownership would be consistent with your business needs and overall plan of succession. Avoiding probate is only one part of the equation.

Let's take the common situation where husband and wife own all of their assets jointly with right of survivorship because they both want the survivor to get everything in the event of death. This is an efficient way to transfer ownership because the surviving joint owner becomes the sole owner with little or no formality. Convenient and appealing as the arrangement may be, joint tenancy cannot be regarded as an "estate plan." In fact, it can have some very unintended consequences in some situations. Here are some considerations to keep in mind.

LACK OF CONTROL AFTER DEATH.

Joint ownership affords no control after your death, as does a living trust or a will with trust provisions. The surviving joint owner becomes the sole owner and can dispose of the assets or money in any manner he or she wishes. This is fine where the surviving joint owner is your spouse, and you have full confidence that what remains will ultimately pass to the desired beneficiaries. But what if your spouse has children by prior marriage, and you wonder whether the step children might influence him or her? If you want to be certain that your estate ultimately goes to your own children or grandchildren rather than stepchildren, either a living trust or a will with trust provisions must be used rather than joint ownership. You lose all control after your death with joint ownership.

UNANTICIPATED TAX CONSEQUENCES.

Unless each joint tenant contributes equally, there can be adverse tax consequences simply by establishing joint ownership. Under current tax laws, there are no tax consequences when you establish joint ownership with your spouse because unlimited gifts can be made to one's spouse with no tax consequence. But there could be surprises in the case of joint ownership with others, depending on the type of asset. Let's assume that you own 100 shares of General Motors. You hold the stock certificate and keep it in a safe deposit box (rather than having it titled in "street-name" at a brokerage firm). You send the certificate to the transfer agent with instructions to add your child's name as a co-owner. A gift has been made when the transfer agent reissues the certificate in both names! That's because you cannot change your mind and take the gift back unless the new owner consents – the transfer agent would require both signatures to put ownership back in your name alone. A gift of one half is considered to have been made when the adverse interest was created.

*Hard feelings can arise between a care-giver child
and the other, non-resident children.*

Jointly-owned real property is similar to a stock certificate in that all owners must sign to transfer title. You cannot create a joint tenancy in real property and unilaterally take it back if you later change your mind – the signature of all co-owners would be required to re-convey jointly-owned real property. As a result of creating this adverse interest in another person, a gift is made for federal gift and estate tax purposes when the joint ownership is created. In either of these examples, a gift tax return (Form 709) would be required if the value of all gifts to the donee during the year exceeded $11,000 (2004 figure). The return is due by April 15th of the following calendar year.

Note, however, that a gift is not made when a joint bank account or joint brokerage account (in street name) is established. That's because the original owner is free to withdraw the funds at any time and undo the "gift" by writing checks on a money market fund. The consent of the new co-owner is not needed, as in the case of real property or stocks where the certificate is held. However, the original owner is deemed to have made a gift if and when the non-contributing joint owner makes a withdrawal from the account.

CARRY-OVER BASIS.

The tax consequence of making a gift is often unexpected. The most common surprise is the carry-over basis. Many people are surprised to learn after the fact about the capital gains tax consequences inherent in gifts. When a completed gift is made, the donee gets what is known as a "carry-over" tax basis in the stock, real estate or other asset. That is, the donee's tax basis is the same as the donor's tax basis. With cash, of course, this is no problem. But if the gifted property is highly appreciated, capital gains tax will be due when the donee sells the property. If the donor is elderly, it is normally preferable from an income tax standpoint to continue to hold the asset until death so that the beneficiary or estate will get a "step-up" in basis to market value. That way, the successor (or estate) can sell it without capital gains tax consequences – i.e., the pre-death appreciation completely escapes capital gains taxation.

EXAMPLE 6.

Tax basis of gifts - Robert was diagnosed with a terminal illnes. His daughter, Susie, came to take care of him during his remaining months so he would not have to go to the nursing home. Robert was very appreciative and wanted her to receive his home – he was leaving it to her in his will anyway. So he deeded the home to Susie a few weeks before his death to avoid probate. Robert had paid $75,000 for the home many years before, but it was worth $300,000 at the time of the gift.

Susie wants to go back to her family after Robert's death and decides to sell the home. She learns for the first time that if she sells the home, she will have to pay capital gains tax on $225,000 because she received a carry-over tax basis with respect to the asset given to her. The only way to avoid capital gains taxation would be to live in the home for two years before selling and claim it as her principal residence.

If Robert had let the home go to her by will, Susie would have received a stepped-up tax basis equal to its value at the time of his death, $300,000 in this example. As a result, Susie would be free to sell the home after his death and pay no capital gains (except, of course, as to any post-death appreciation).

Susie would also get a step-up in basis if Robert had given her the home but retained a life estate – Susie's tax basis would be $300,000 after his death.

MISCHIEF.

I have seen many instances where a joint account is established as a matter of convenience with a child who lives locally, with the understanding that the child will pay the bills in the event of incompetency and divide the remainder equally with his or her siblings after death (or with no "understanding" at all). Fortunately, most children keep their word, and the decedent's wishes are fulfilled. But not always. Sometimes, the local child who provided most of the care during the last months or years of the parent's life starts to resent the lost income and feels entitled to more. The legal reality is that the surviving child becomes the sole owner of the account or asset upon death and can do with it as he or she pleases. Although many states have a presumption by statute that the funds in a joint account remain the property of the person who contributed them, this presumption typically ceases upon the death of the contributing joint owner. The funds then belong to the surviving joint owner. The other siblings might have some evidence indicating that the parent wanted them to share the account, and they might have some legal theories to support the contention. But they would have the burden of proof, and it would be an uphill battle. The outcome of litigation would be in doubt, and the legal cost would be sufficiently high that litigation could be seriously considered only where the sums at stake were large.

Underlying these considerations is the risk that the joint owner can and sometimes does withdraw funds before death. This causes ill will, if not hardship, within the family. If the errant joint owner refuses to return the funds, the only recourse is to bring a lawsuit. As said, many states give the contributing joint owner a presumption that the funds are still his or hers, but no one likes to take the drastic measure of suing another family member. Lawsuits are seldom brought for the additional reason that the elder joint owner is often aged, feeble and afraid of alienating someone upon whom he or she feels dependent.

SIMULTANEOUS DEATH.

Joint tenancy does not necessarily avoid probate where there is a simultaneous death. Under the Uniform Simultaneous Death Act in force in most states, if both owners – husband and wife, let's say – perish simultaneously or under circumstances where it cannot be determined who died first, such as a plane crash, half would pass as though one spouse died first and half would pass as though the other spouse died first. If wills existed, the terms of the will would govern and half of the joint account proceeds would be added to the probate estate of each spouse.

If this couple did not have wills, half would go to the heirs at law of each spouse. This might not have been their wish, particularly if the heirs are distant relatives. Or, if the heirs happened to be minor children, a court-supervised guardianship or conservatorship would probably be required until they reach legal age, which should be avoided due to the expense and also due to the relatively young age at which the children would receive the remaining balance – eighteen in many states. This outcome can be easily averted by nominating a guardian in your will and directing that your estate be distributed to a trust for the benefit of the minor children. The guardian could also serve as trustee, or you could name a third party to serve as trustee.

INCAPACITY.

Let's assume that you deed your home to yourself and your child as joint owners with right of survivorship. You want your child to get the home, and joint ownership with survivorship looks like a good way to avoid probate. The home has not appreciated in value, so capital gains would not be a problem. Then your health fails, and funds are needed for your cost of care. As already explained, all joint owners must sign in order to sell real property. As long as all joint owners are willing and able to sign, this presents no problem. But if a child balks, you will not be able to sell it. If you are no longer competent, a guardian or conservator might have to be appointed to pursue litigation in order to deal with the recalcitrant child – just hope that he or she has not filed for bankruptcy or divorce in the meantime!

Similarly, if the parent has since become incompetent, a court-supervised guardianship or conservatorship might be required just to get authority for someone to sign the deed on behalf of the incompetent person. This would be the case even if the child is willing to cooperate by signing the deed (although the empowerment question might be satisfied if a properly drafted durable power of attorney had been executed while still competent).

BANKRUPTCY.

A trustee in bankruptcy can have rights in property superior to the joint owner who filed for bankruptcy! It could become a disaster if you make someone a joint owner in an asset, and he or she later files for bankruptcy.

FEDERAL ESTATE TAXATION.

Joint ownership can be a major disadvantage when federal estate taxes are a consideration. If the combined estates of both spouses exceeds the federal estate tax exemption ($1.5 million in 2004 and 2005), trust wills (or living trusts with tax provisions) are needed in order to get the benefit of one federal estate tax exemption for each spouse. Owning everything jointly could deprive your ultimate beneficiaries of two exemptions because the surviving owner (rather than the trust) becomes the sole owner. Even if the surviving spouse were to disclaim, this could result in additional estate taxes of up to $675,000 (2004 rates) when the surviving spouse dies, depending, of course, on the size of the state and the tax rate in effect when the surviving spouse dies.

JOINT BROKERAGE ACCOUNTS – POST-DEATH.

Stock brokerage firms all offer joint accounts with right of survivorship. These accounts are a very popular form of ownership, particularly between spouses, because probate is avoided. After the death of one joint owner, the surviving owner becomes the sole owner of the account upon satisfactory proof of death, such as a death certificate.

However, the process is not fully automatic. Upon being notified of the death of one joint account owner, a brokerage firm will "freeze" the account so that no more orders can be processed. Limit orders to buy or sell will be cancelled. No more checks can be written on the cash or money market accounts. After the brokerage firm receives a certified copy of the death certificate, an affidavit of domicile (form provided by brokerage firm), and instructions from the surviving joint owner or owners, it will liquidate the securities or transfer them to a new account or follow whatever instructions are given by the surviving joint owners. In some cases, the brokerage firm will want estate and state inheritance tax releases.

EXAMPLE 7.

Joint brokerage account frozen - Fred opened a joint account at his brokerage firm with his two children. He later passed away. Upon learning of his death, the brokerage firm froze the account. All pending limit orders to buy or sell were cancelled, and no withdrawals could be made to the account. Later that month, his children brought in a certified copy of the death certificate and other documentation requested by the brokerage firm. They instructed the stocks to be sold and each received half of the proceeds.

JOINT BANK ACCOUNTS – POST-DEATH.

Banks also have joint accounts with right of survivorship, but they are handled differently from joint accounts with a brokerage firm. A bank is not concerned about the death of a joint owner and will not freeze the account. Any surviving joint owner can continue to write checks or withdraw funds as though there had been no death (assuming the account was set up so that either could sign).

EXAMPLE 8.

Joint bank account not frozen -Take the previous example, where Fred wants his children to divide what remains equally after his death without probate. Fred set up a joint checking account at his bank with himself and his two children as joint owners. After his death, one child went into the bank and withdrew the entire balance. The bank knew about Fred's passing and suspected that he wanted both children to share equally. However, the bank felt that it had no choice but to honor the request to withdraw – to do otherwise would be breach of contract! Had the account been with a brokerage firm, the account would have been frozen until both children agreed on instructions. In this case Fred could have left the bank account in his name and signed a "pay-on-death" rider, which gives the balance to his children after his death but no ownership rights before death. That way, the children would have shared equally upon presentation of a death certificate. A probate would be avoided without the risk of unintended consequences.

SUMMARY.

Joint ownership is not always as simple as it may seem. I always advise clients that it is fine to have a family checking account in joint account form because it provides some immediate liquidity in the event of death or incapacity. Except in the case of spouses wanting the balance to go to the survivor outright, the bulk of one's estate should not normally be held in joint ownership. Joint tenancy is not an estate plan or estate plan substitute. Joint tenancy has probably been responsible for frustrating the testamentary wishes of more people than any other single cause. It can easily result in an overall distribution that is quite contrary to the deceased person's intent. Use it with care!

CHAPTER FOUR

ANNUITIES

This chapter deals with another common way of avoiding probate – annuities. There are two basic types of annuities – fixed annuities and variable annuities. Although both are referred to as annuities, fixed annuities and variable annuities are inherently quite different. Fixed annuities are far more common with seniors.

FIXED ANNUITIES.

Fixed annuities are very popular with seniors, not to mention those who sell them and earn a nice commission! Seniors view them as "nest eggs" which will always be available in case of need. Annuities look like a good deal because they are tax-deferred, and the interest is not taxed unless and until a withdrawal is made. If the owner is over age 59½, the ten per cent income tax penalty for early withdrawal does not apply.

A fixed annuity is an unsecured contract between an insurance company and the policy holder. The insurance company agrees to pay interest for a specified term of years, and then pay back the principal and any accrued interest that was not previously withdrawn. Although the terms and conditions vary with each insurance company and annuity contract, an annuity typically contains a provision imposing a "surrender charge" or "early withdrawal penalty" for withdrawal prior to the end of the term. The surrender charge often diminishes each year until it reaches zero in five years or seven years. However, I have seen policies that impose severe penalties over longer periods. Many annuity policies allow the owner to withdraw up to 10% of the principal each year without incurring a surrender charge.

At the end of the contract period, the owner has the option of continuing to defer by renewing the annuity, or of taking a lump sum payment, or of "annuitizing;" i.e., taking payments over a period of years or for life. Annuities frequently offer an initial rate of return which is above market, but the "teaser rate" usually falls to market rate after one year. The longer the term of the annuity, the more important the financial strength of the insurance company becomes.

These various features appeal to many seniors because they figure "it will always be there if I need it," and "I don't have to pay income tax on the earnings unless and until I withdraw." Most of them ignore the fact that they pay little income tax anyway.

Annuities look appealing, but there are some tax disadvantages which are not so apparent. First of all, the fallacy in focusing on the tax deferral aspect is that if you ever do need the funds, the investment ceases to be tax-deferred. If and when you withdraw funds, the interest portion of the withdrawal will be subject to federal income tax and possibly state income tax as well. You will have derived little or no benefit from the deferral of taxes because the interest portion will always be taxed when withdrawn. In the end, the "tax-deferred nest egg" reasoning holds water only if you have an offsetting income tax deduction, such as very high medical expenses, in the year of liquidation.

On the other hand, if you never do need the funds and pass away, the account balance will pass to your named beneficiaries upon your death pursuant to the beneficiary designation. The benefits to them of tax deferral are questionable to non-existent in most cases. Although probate is avoided by the beneficiary designation feature, the tax deferral usually ceases at time of death. If the beneficiary opts to take cash (which they almost always do), he or she will be taxed on *all* the accrued interest in the year of receipt. The insurance company will issue IRS Form 1099 the following January, and the interest portion will get added to the beneficiary's other taxable income and most likely be taxed at a higher marginal rate. As a result, a high portion of the interest will go to state and federal income taxes. The beneficiary could avoid bunching all the taxable interest into one year by electing a payment option other than lump-sum cash, but they seldom do so. The point is that the interest earned by an annuity will always be taxed to the recipient when it is paid out, and it will be taxed at ordinary rates, not capital gains rates.

EXAMPLE 9.

Annuity - taxation of accumulated income -Assume that an individual purchased an annuity for $100,000 and it increased in value over the years to $150,000, due to accumulated interest. Income taxes have never been paid on the accumulated interest. That $50,000 will *always be taxed as ordinary income* — it's just a question of when it gets taxed and who pays it. If the recipient is a charity, it would not matter because the charity does not pay income taxes. But assume that the beneficiary is the owner's adult child, who is already in the 33% tax bracket. Upon the death of the annuity owner, the child would, upon receipt of the $150,000, pay more than $16,500 in federal income taxes on the $50,000 of accumulated interest (and possibly state and city income taxes, depending on where the beneficiary lives).

The total tax bill on annuity interest will normally be minimized if the retired parent withdraws the interest each year and pays income tax on it at his or her lower rates. Take away the tax deferral aspect, and a fixed annuity resembles a U. S. savings bond. Except that an annuity is not guaranteed by the federal government as is a U.S. savings bond. In addition, annuity income is subject to state income tax.

The case for annuities gets even weaker for estates large enough to be subject to the federal estate tax. It's almost a case of double taxation, due to the income tax concept known as "income in respect of a decedent." If the estate in the above example was subject to federal estate taxes, the *full* $150,000 would be included in the gross estate for federal estate tax purposes. In addition, the beneficiary will pay income tax on the $50,000 of accrued interest! The beneficiary would get a small break on his individual income tax return in that he could deduct the *extra* estate tax that was paid as a result of the accrued interest on the annuity. However, this is only a deduction, not a credit. A credit would be a dollar-for-dollar offset, whereas a deduction results in a tax savings of only 31%, or whatever his tax bracket happens to be.

EXAMPLE 10.
Estate & income taxation of annuities - Assume that the estate in Example 9 is taxable in the lowest estate tax bracket of 45% (2004 rate). At the lowest estate tax rate, the estate would have paid an extra $22,500 in estate taxes as a result of the $50,000 of accumulated interest (45% X $50,000). The

son gets a deduction of $22,500 on his personal income tax return for the additional estate taxes paid on the interest portion, but this saves him only $7,425 ($22,500 X 33%). The total tax bill in this example is as follows:

Federal estate tax on $100,000 investment	$45,000
Federal estate tax on $50,000 accrued interest	22,500
Federal income tax on $27,500	
($50,000 less $22,500) @ 33%	9,075
	$76,575

This beneficiary would be much happier to have inherited appreciated stock or real property worth $150,000, as to which he would enjoy a stepped-up basis and could sell with *no* income tax consequences! The value of an asset will always be included in the gross taxable estate of the parent, but the $9,075 of income taxes would have been avoided. Tax deferral does little to benefit the parent and normally only results in transferring the interest income onto the successor's Form 1040. The tax bite will usually be lower if the deceased annuity owner withdraws interest annually rather than allowing it to build up and be bunched up in one year on the beneficiary's return.

Although annuities are often an undesirable vehicle for passing wealth to the next generation, they do have a legitimate use as a means of providing income. A person with limited means can purchase an immediate-payout annuity and receive a known monthly income for life or for life with a guaranteed minimum period of time, such as ten years. A payout annuity will at least give some peace of mind in, addition to providing a stream of income.

Annuities can also be used to good advantage where a child is a spendthrift or unable to manage finances and where the estate is too small to warrant the expense of a professional trustee. The executor or successor trustee is directed in the will or trust agreement to buy an annuity and elect an irrevocable settlement option so that the beneficiary will get a monthly check from the insurance company for life or a period of years. This is a more cost-effective method than a trust for extending control after death where the amounts do not justify the cost of a trustee.

Annuities can also be used to help pay for college costs for grandchildren – direct the executor, for example, to purchase four annuities for each grandchild – one due when the child enters college, one when a sophomore, etc. Or, one annuity with annual or quarterly payments. However, if you want built-in flexibility for lump sum distributions that might be needed but cannot be anticipated, such as unknown medical needs or buying a first home or getting started in a business, then you need a trust. A settlement option on an annuity offers only a schedule of payments. The same lack of flexibility would be felt if the grandchild decided not to go to college – the payout terms of the annuity contract would prevail.

An annuity can occasionally be used to help someone needing skilled nursing care to qualify for Medicaid assistance. If the proper irrevocable payout option is elected and the stream of payments is not assignable, countable assets can be converted into income by purchasing an annuity for the well spouse, without affecting the eligibility of the ill spouse. These situations are somewhat infrequent, and the success of this strategy varies by state. See Chapter 14 for details on annuities in the Medicaid context.

Lastly, every investor should bear in mind that an annuity is no more than an unsecured contract with an insurance company. You pay your money, and the company gives you a piece of paper which is a contract. If the insurance company mismanages its assets or runs into financial problems, insolvency becomes a possibility. The annuity may be guaranteed by an affiliated company of the issuer, in which case you need to look at the financial strength of the guarantor. The longer the term of the annuity, of course, the more important the financial strength of the company. Every annuity investor should be careful to deal only with a company that is financially sound. Check the company's rating with Weiss, A. M. Best, Fitch, Moody's and/or Standard & Poors. It's difficult to compare the rating of one agency with another, so here is a table that should be helpful:

Insurance companies receive report cards

Five companies grade insurers' strengths, but each uses different criteria. When you buy a new policy or annuity, choose an insurer rated secure by at least three of the five ratings companies.

COMPANY	RANGES		
	SECURE	VULNERABLE	POOR
A.M. Best			
www.ambest.com	A++ to B+	B to C-	D to F
Fitch Ratings			
www.fitchratings.com	AAA to BBB-	BB+ to C	DDD to D
Moody's Investors Services			
www.moodys.com	Aaa to Baa3	Ba1 to B3	Caa1 to C
Standard & Poor's			
www.standardandpoors.com	AAA to BBB-	BB+ to CCC-	CC to R
Weiss Ratings			
www.weissratings.com	A+ to C-	D+ to D-	E+ to F

VARIABLE ANNUITIES.

A variable annuity is another type of contract with an insurance company. They appeal to some investors because you can invest in mutual funds and your named beneficiaries will never receive less than you invested. It's basically a mutual fund backed up with contingent life insurance to pay back your original investment if you die and the value of the investments in the account happens to be less than your original investment at the time of your death. The investments are held in the name of the annuity owner and monthly or quarterly statements are sent which show the performance of the investments. Like fixed annuities, variable annuities are tax deferred.

Variable annuities look like a good deal to those who want to invest in mutual funds because you get to invest in stock or bond mutual funds, and the named beneficiaries will never receive less than you invested. Since the investment is tax deferred, you pay no income tax unless and until you withdraw. However, there is no guaranteed rate of return as in the case of a fixed annuity. Plus you, the investor, run the risk of a decrease in value if you need to withdraw funds during your lifetime.

The main problem with variable annuities is the high expense ratio. The life insurance component only covers a drop in value between investment and death, and you pay dearly for it. A high proportion of the expected annual return, whatever it may turn out to be, goes to pay for the life insurance component. This is in addition to the normal expenses associated with a comparable mutual fund. The high expenses will make a huge difference when compounded over the years. In this writer's opinion, variable annuities should be considered only when there is some specific reason to want both tax deferral and a mutual fund.

LIFE INSURANCE.

Life insurance perhaps should not even be included at this point in the discussion because life insurance is usually not chosen as an investment vehicle to avoid probate. However, you should have a clear understanding of the differences between life insurance and annuities, both of which are contracts with a life insurance company. A life insurance policy does pass the policy proceeds directly to the named beneficiaries, and it is similar to a fixed annuity in several respects. Like a fixed annuity, a life insurance policy is an unsecured contract with an insurance company. It is similar to a fixed annuity in other respects: the earnings build up within the policy, and the owner can name a beneficiary to receive the proceeds directly after the insured's death. The insurance company will pay the policy proceeds to the named beneficiary after death of the insured, without probate and free of creditor claims, upon receipt of a death certificate. However, there are significant differences between a life insurance policy and an annuity, of which one should be aware.

Annuities can be used to good advantage where a child is unable to manage finances.

Life insurance proceeds receive preferential treatment under income tax law. Take Example 9, where $100,000 was invested in an annuity which grew to $150,000 and the $50,000 of deferred income is taxed to the recipient as ordinary income. If the same $100,000 lump sum had been invested in a single-premium life insurance policy with $150,000 face value, the $50,000 build-up in value within the policy would never be subjected to income tax. The growth is tax-free rather than tax-deferred. The beneficiary would receive policy proceeds of $150,000, and there would be virtually no income tax liability. In this respect, a life insurance policy is strikingly different from a deferred annuity.

The two, of course, are not strictly comparable investment options because a senior considering an annuity might not be insurable or it might be too expensive. And a lump sum investment of $100,000 might not buy $150,000 of coverage, depending on the age and health of the person whose life is to be insured.

CHAPTER FIVE

OTHER METHODS OF AVOIDING PROBATE

Various and sundry other ways existing to avoid probate.

PAY-ON-DEATH ACCOUNTS.

Most states have adopted the Uniform Transfer on Death Act. Banks and credit unions offer "pay on death" arrangements which have the advantage of allowing the account owner to retain full ownership and control during lifetime while at the same time avoiding probate after death. You open the account in your name and under your Social Security number and name your beneficiaries on a pay-on-death rider. You can change beneficiaries any time you wish (as long as you are competent, of course!) The advantage of this type of account is that, unlike joint accounts, the prospective beneficiaries cannot withdraw funds prior to your death.

Their signature is not needed to open the account; in fact, they won't even know the account exists unless you tell them! The obvious advantage is that funds go to the beneficiaries after death without probate, but the beneficiaries are never subjected to temptation because they have no access to the funds during your lifetime.

Pay-on-death riders are also useful in situations where a couple has a joint account and are concerned about a possible simultaneous death. They can name their living trust or their children as pay-on-death beneficiaries and avoid having the funds tied up by probate.

Accounts of this type are known as Totten trusts in some states.

TRANSFER ON DEATH.

Stock brokerage firms have essentially the same type of account as the pay-on-death account offered by banks and credit unions, except that it is known under the enabling laws as "transfer on death."

BENEFICIARY DEEDS.

Numerous states have passed legislation allowing assets with registered title (cars, boats, trailers, planes, and, in a few states, even the home) to be left to individuals without probate. The property can be left to more than one person as joint tenants or as tenants in common. Since it is revocable, a beneficiary deed can be revoked or changed. Unlike joint ownership, the designee does not acquire any ownership rights prior to death of the grantor or surviving grantor. The beneficiary deed must be filed or recorded with the designated authority prior to death and is conceptually similar to pay-on-death and transfer-on-death designations, except that it applies to titled assets rather than to cash and securities.

SMALL ESTATE AFFIDAVIT.

Most states have enacted legislation which allows small estates to be transferred to a deceased person's heirs at law or beneficiaries of a will by the expedience of an affidavit. It is an abbreviated form of probate, because expenses of last illness, creditors and taxing authorities still must be paid out of the assets. The small estate affidavit procedure is much less costly because it avoids most of the formalities and expense of probate. If someone passes away owning a small parcel of real property or a bank account that was not jointly owned or had not been transferred to the living trust, for instance, the small estate affidavit procedure would be a good way to avoid a full probate. The asset or assets would be transferred to the beneficiaries named in the will (or heirs at law, if there was no will) following the procedure set forth in the state's statute. But – unlike joint ownership, pay-on-death, annuities, etc. – the creditors would have to be paid in the process. The small estate affidavit acts do not affect who inherits – that is governed either by the will or by the laws of intestacy if there is no will.

The requirements for using small estate affidavits are different in every state. The shortcoming of small estate affidavits is that the maximum dollar limits in most states tends to be quite low, sometimes as low as $10,000. Since there is no court supervision, affidavits afford less protection for creditors and other beneficiaries, and the state legislatures have been slow to raise the ceiling amounts.

LIVING TRUSTS.

Living trusts are a popular way of avoiding probate in many states. A "living trust," as used in this book, refers to a revocable trust established by someone during his or her lifetime. Since they are a major topic, Part III is devoted entirely to revocable living trusts.

PART III

Living Trusts

CHAPTER SIX

TRUSTS

A trust is a three-party arrangement, contractual in nature, whereby one person (the trustor) transfers property to another person (the trustee) for the benefit of a third party (the beneficiary). Trusts are very flexible and can serve many useful purposes. They have been recognized for centuries and are effective vehicles for both lifetime planning and estate planning. This chapter will focus on the basics of revocable living trusts and the situations in which they are useful.

GLOSSARY OF TRUST TERMS.

There are many different types of trusts and the terminology which should be understood:

Trustor, settlor or grantor - These are synonyms referencing the person who establishes the trust and transfers assets to it. The choice of term will vary with the attorney drafting the trust agreement.

Trustee - The trustee is a fiduciary who manages the trust assets pursuant to the directions set forth in the trust agreement and applicable law. Fiduciaries are subject to various fiduciary duties that are discussed in Appendix C.

Beneficiary - The beneficiary is the person or class of persons for whose benefit the trust exists. Often there is more than one class of beneficiaries, such as income beneficiaries and remaindermen, who get what remains when the trust terminates.

Intervivos trust - An intervivos trust is one that is set up during the lifetime of the trustor (as opposed to a testamentary trust, which is set up by will). An intervivos trust can be either revocable or irrevocable.

Revocable trust - A revocable trust is an intervivos trust which by its terms can be amended, revoked or terminated by the trustor while living and competent. The term "living trust" usually refers to a revocable intervivos trust which the trustor sets up, naming himself (or himself and spouse) as lifetime beneficiary and either himself, his spouse or a third party as trustee.

Self-administered living trust, or "SALT" In a self-administered living trust, the trustor names himself (or himself and spouse) as trustee. The trustor and spouse are usually the beneficiaries as well. Upon the incompetence or death of one or both, a successor trustee takes over.

Irrevocable trust - This is an intervivos trust that the trustor cannot revoke or amend. The trustor has parted with control over the money or assets transferred to the trust. The trust is thereafter managed by the trustee for the beneficiaries according to the terms of the trust. A gift tax return (Form 709) might have to be filed, depending on the value of the assets transferred to the trust.

Testamentary trust - A testamentary trust is one which is set up by a will. The property subject to the will is probated, and upon completion of probate, the executor distributes the assets to the trustee. A testamentary trust by its very nature requires probate; it does not avoid probate.

Credit shelter or bypass trust - These are synonyms for a trust which is established to utilize two federal estate tax exemptions, one for each spouse. A trust of this type can be established either as a living trust or as a testamentary trust. These trusts are explained in greater detail in Chapter 10.

Grantor trust - This is a term of art under the income tax code. The income tax consequences of the trust are imputed back to the trustor, or grantor, who established the trust.

Charitable trust - A trust established to benefit a charity and frequently another beneficiary, such as the trustor or trustor and spouse. There are many different types of charitable trusts, the most common of which are discussed in Chapter 11.

Irrevocable life insurance trust - A trust established to own a life insurance policy and receive the proceeds upon the death of the insured. See page 113.

Special needs trust - A trust established to benefit a disabled person who is eligible for public assistance of some type or types. Also known as supplemental needs trust.

Support trust - A trust established to support the beneficiary or beneficiaries. The trust agreement could require the trustee to distribute all income, or all income plus whatever principal the trustee thinks advisable for the beneficiary. It could also leave the question totally to the discretion of the trustee. The trust agreement would also specify what the distributions are to be made for, the most common purposes being support or support and education.

Sprinkle trust - A trust with more than one beneficiary, where the trustee has discretion to distribute according to need.

Generation-skipping trust - A trust which is established for the benefit of grandchildren to take advantage of the generation-skipping exemption and reduce federal estate taxes.

Dynasty trust - For centuries the rule against perpetuities has restricted the length of time for which assets can be tied up in a trust, such as a life in being plus twenty one years, or two lives in being. States are starting to eliminate the rule against perpetuities, which paves the way for very large trusts which can last for many generations, or conceivably forever.

Many of these special trusts are beyond the scope of this book and are not discussed further.

LIFETIME PLANNING.

Trusts serve an incredibly wide variety of needs, the most common of which will be discussed in this chapter. Trust uses fall into three broad categories:

- **Lifetime planning** - for self or others.

- **Extending control after death.**

- **Minimizing succession transfer costs** - avoiding probate, reducing estate and inheritance taxes.

To realize lifetime planning benefits of a trust, you must establish an intervivos, or "living" trust. Extending control after death can be accomplished either with an intervivos trust or with a testamentary trust; i.e., one which is established by will. Use of trusts and trust wills to reduce estate and inheritance taxes is discussed separately in Part IV, Taxable Estates.

Avoiding probate can be a major motivation for choosing a trust.

Disability planning for yourself. Lifetime planning is, in this author's opinion, one of the foremost reasons for choosing a trust rather than a will as one's principal estate planning vehicle. A trust has no equal for lifetime planning because, when well-conceived and drafted, it will provide comprehensive instructions to the named trustee or successor trustee in the event of incapacity. This could avoid thousands of dollars of legal expense for a court-supervised conservatorship or guardianship to handle income and assets. Even if probate costs are minimal in your state, a trust should be considered as a way to reduce the risk of a future conservatorship for managing income and assets.

Most people loathe the thought of going to a nursing home. Someone concerned that he or she might become incompetent as a result of a disabling disease or condition that runs in the family and also determined not to end up in a nursing home should give consideration to a living trust. If your net worth is large enough to bear the cost, you can get quite creative in giving special directions to your successor trustee in the event of your incapacity. For instance, you can instruct your successor trustee to spend trust funds liberally to keep you out of the nursing home as long as possible:

- Spend your trust money generously so that you can remain at home as long as possible, regardless of cost, including 24-hour care.

- Hire a geriatric care manager to prepare a plan of care, to include physical therapy, rehabilitation therapy, speech and language therapy and medical-social services, over and above what Medicare provides.

- Provide that if you are hospitalized or have to go to a nursing home as a last resort, the trustee is to pay the cost of extra amenities, such as:

A private room

Extra care givers

Someone to monitor the quality of care you receive

Don't sell your home until necessary

- Hire a personal attorney to monitor your situation to make sure your wishes in your trust agreement are followed. The trust pays.

- Arrange and pay for companions to visit with you, read to you, play your favorite music.

- Hire someone to cook the special foods you like.

- Arrange for domestic chores, such as cleaning; cooking; shopping for food and medicine; transportation for medical appointments, 24-hour care and the like. The trustee is directed to pay the cost.

- Name an individual and a bank to serve as co-trustees. The bank or trust company handles the money and the individual gives advice on how to spend it.

These amenities would be important to many people, particularly people without a spouse or nearby children to rely on. If you are fortunate enough to have the means to pay for special care, a specially-drafted trust is needed to assure that your well being will be promoted in the manner you wish. The reason I say "specially-drafted" is that most trust agreements are not drafted with such considerations in mind. Most attorneys draft trust agreements simply to avoid probate or to establish a credit shelter trust to assure that two exemptions are available for federal estate tax purposes, one for each spouse. If you want extraordinary steps taken to keep you out of the nursing home, you need to give your successor trustee specific written instructions. Unless the trust instrument makes explicit provision as to how your money should be spent in the event of your disability or incapacity, there is a significant risk that the successor trustee will not spend trust funds generously to accomplish your objectives. Here's why:

You as trustor/trustee/beneficiary, of course, can spend the trust income and principal in any manner you wish. However, if your health fails and you become incapacitated, you obviously will not be able to continue as trustee. The successor trustee named in the trust agreement will take over. A bank, trust company or other successor trustee might be reluctant to spend trust money for the special purposes set forth above unless the trust agreement clearly directs it. An institutional trustee will be concerned that the children or other remaindermen might later contend that the expenditures were extravagant and unauthorized. If there is any grumbling about the expenditures being extravagant or unauthorized, the bank will immediately feel the inherent conflict in its dual duty to both the remaindermen and the lifetime beneficiary. A bank as trustee has a duty to both the remaindermen and the lifetime beneficiary. A decision in favor of the lifetime beneficiary often is contrary to the best interests of the remaindermen; and vice versa. The last thing a bank or trust company wants is a later claim by the remaindermen that the expenditures were unauthorized and that the excess should be repaid with the bank's own funds. It will err on the side of caution in making distributions.

You can steer clear of this dilemma by giving clear directions in the trust agreement as to how your funds are to be spent – then the bank will simply be following orders. Give your successor trustee a safe harbor by making your wishes explicit.

Note that this conflict between the lifetime beneficiary and remaindermen is not necessarily overcome by naming one child as successor trustee rather than a bank or trust company. Even if the trustee child knows your wishes and would be inclined to follow them, there is the same risk that the other children as remaindermen could make the same claim against sibling serving as successor trustee – unauthorized expenditures! A bank would be a more inviting target, of course, than a sibling, but the possibility is still there.

In short, if you have a living trust or are considering one and would want your money spent in some of the special ways discussed above, make certain that the trust agreement clearly states that your lifetime needs are to prevail over the rights of the other beneficiaries. Think the situation through, and state your wishes clearly right in the trust agreement. The more fractious the family, the more important clear instructions become.

EXTENDING CONTROL AFTER DEATH.

There can be very legitimate reasons for wanting to extend control of your estate beyond the grave. Without a trust, your estate will be distributed outright to your heirs at law or to the beneficiaries named in your will, individual retirement account, annuity or the like. The recipients will be able to do with the money as they please. In many cases this would be exactly what you would want. But in other instances, an outright gift could range from being improvident in some situations to unthinkable in others.

Providing for spouse. It often happens that one spouse or the other has no interest or experience in managing income and assets. A trust is an excellent way to arrange for the financial expertise that will be needed after the death or incapacity of the manager spouse. If this is your primary concern and you have misgivings about someone's judgment, you can set up an intervivos trust and see how the person does as trustee. If he or she makes poor decisions, you can name a new trustee.

Protecting spendthrifts. Maybe one of the objects of your bounty is a big spender – always out of money, lots of credit card debt, can't hold a job, etc. On the one hand, you do not want to disinherit that beneficiary entirely; but on the other hand, you hate the thought of him or her squandering everything in a few months or furthering a life style with which you do not agree. If the dollar amount earmarked for that beneficiary is significant, a trust is the answer! The trustee is given explicit instructions as to what distributions can be made and under what circumstances, and even, if you so desired, discretion as to when the trust is to terminate. In almost all cases where there is an income beneficiary and remaindermen, the trust agreement will contain a spendthrift clause which prohibits any attempt by the beneficiaries to borrow against their interest in the trust.

The situation can be handled similarly where the concern is your child's spouse rather than your child. If your in-law is the big spender and the marriage does not appear to be very stable, you might be concerned about a later divorce. In most states, an inheritance remains the separate property of the recipient, but only so long as it is not commingled with marital assets. Maybe your concern is that your son-in-law or daughter-in-law would successfully pressure your child into putting the inheritance into a joint account or commingling it with marital assets. In the event of divorce, the divorce court might treat it as a marital asset to be divided between the spouses. The chance of this happening could be diminished by use of a trust (although it must be noted that even with a trust, a divorce court inclined to award more assets to your in-law could always give the trust to your child and more of the other assets to the in-law). To best protect the child's interest in the trust in the event of a divorce, the trust agreement could provide for mandatory distribution of only the income. It could give the child the right to give the income or principal, or part of it, to his or her spouse by will, if the marriage survived.

Providing for minor children or grandchildren. People with young children should consider a trust as a way to provide for the support and education of young children. In the case of parents with minor children, this is most commonly done in their wills. The wills give the assets to the surviving spouse, if any; otherwise, the assets go to a trustee for the children. Although this could also be accomplished via a living trust, the risk of both parents dying simultaneously is quite remote. So most younger couples prefer wills rather than setting up and funding a living trust.

Grandparents wanting to help grandchildren with college costs might be inclined to use an annuity or Uniform Transfers to Minors account for smaller sums, and, for larger amounts, to set up a trust, either during lifetime or by will. They also have the option of adding the contribution to a trust or minors account already set up by the parents.

Providing for disabled children. Many disabled people are not self-supporting and cannot live independently. They often cannot not handle their own finances. And the physical and mental condition as well as the earning ability of a disabled person can change over time. In addition to the financial concerns, parents of such children are often faced with the question of who will make residential and healthcare decisions on the child's behalf after both parents are gone? A trust with a responsible trustee is an ideal solution to the financial aspects of these special situations.

If the disabled person is qualified for Supplemental Security Income (SSI) from the Social Security Administration, a special needs trust will be required, also known as a supplemental needs trust. These trusts give the trustee special instructions for making distributions. Competent legal counsel is a necessity where a disabled beneficiary is receiving public assistance and you want to maintain his or her eligibility. If the trust is improperly worded or the distribution instructions are not followed, the disabled person could lose eligibility for his or her public benefits, such as SSI, Food Stamps, Medicaid, and the like. Disabled people are often qualified for more than one assistance program and the programs have differing eligibility standards, which makes it imperative that competent legal counsel be sought.

In most cases parents can make better spending decisions for a disabled child than a third party and want to continue doing so as long as possible. As a result, parents commonly leave their estates to the surviving spouse and provide for the disabled child with contingent trust provisions in their wills, in case of a simultaneous death. Again, it is critical that the instructions to the trustee with respect to distributions be in compliance with the regulations for the public assistance programs for which the disabled child qualifies.

In these situations it is sometimes a problem finding a good trustee to serve when neither parent can. Siblings of the disabled child often live elsewhere or are not inclined to serve, and peers of the parents are also getting old. Some states have pooled trusts administered by a nonprofit organization which provide another option, particularly where the amounts are relatively small.

Second marriages. Couples with children from a prior marriage face a difficult dilemma. They typically want to provide for their spouse in some manner and to leave what remains after the spouse's death to their children. If they leave the estate outright to the spouse, there is no absolute guarantee that the remainder will go to the children of the first marriage on the death of the spouse – the spouse could change his or her will or get married to a high roller and succumb to the pressure to spend. Or lose it through poor decisions. Or leave it to stepchildren.

With some couples the level of mutual trust is so high that they feel comfortable with an understanding that what remains will be disposed of in an agreed way and will not be changed after the first death. People having a need for more certainty will have to think in terms of a trust. A trust can be utilized to provide for the surviving spouse during his or her lifetime and upon death to have the remainder distributed to the trustor's natural children. This is another situation that calls for competent legal counsel, particularly if the estates are large enough to owe estate or inheritance taxes.

MINIMIZING SUCCESSION TRANSFER COSTS.

Avoiding Probate. One attribute of a trust, of course, is that it avoids probate. In states where the cost of probate is high, avoiding probate can be a major motivation for choosing a trust rather than a will. In the typical case of a husband and wife, this being their only marriage and both wanting everything to go to the surviving spouse and then to the children and with both spouses being able to handle finances, a self-administered revocable living trust is ideal. In this situation, you want the assets to be transferred to the surviving spouse and ultimate beneficiaries as efficiently as possible. A revocable living trust will not avoid the need to pay creditors and expenses of last illness. Nor will it avoid the need to file final income tax returns and possibly estate or inheritance tax returns. But in states with high probate costs, the remaining assets will pass to the ultimate beneficiaries with less legal expense using a revocable living trust rather than a will. Plus, it can avoid a conservatorship.

On the other hand, if the cost of probate in your state is minimal, it might cost more to set up and fund a trust than to do a probate!

Ownership of real property in other states. Living trusts can be used to particular advantage where real property is owned in more than one state. Someone owning real property in another state is an ideal candidate for a living trust. If the decedent died a resident of one state and did not have a trust, the main probate proceeding would be there. In addition, an "ancillary probate" would be necessary in every other state in which real property was owned. Ancillary probate procedures are usually more streamlined than the main probate, so the cost should be less. But it doesn't always work out that way. The cost of an ancillary probate can be significant. Many a client has been surprised at the bill when dealing with an out-of-state attorney on a one-time matter!

I recall one couple who owned substantial rental property in one state, plus a ranch in a second state and another ranch in a third state. They had one daughter who was the ultimate beneficiary. Due to the real estate, they were potentially looking at six probates someday - two in State A, two in State B and two in State C. The number of probates could be reduced from six to three if the couple used joint ownership (or tenancy by the entireties), but one probate and two ancillary probates would still be necessary upon the death of the second parent in order to transfer the estate to the daughter. By using a living trust, all probates were eliminated and a significant potential expense avoided. The disadvantage of this approach was the added expense to set up a trust and retain an attorney in the other states to convey the real property. But that expense was far less than ancillary probates would be.

CHAPTER SEVEN

FUNDING OF LIVING TRUSTS

Working out the details and executing a trust agreement is only half of the equation! A revocable living trust also has to be "funded" by transferring assets to the trustee. If this all-important step is not taken, a probate might be needed, even though a trust agreement exists!

I have seen many instances where a trust agreement was signed, but the home, for instance, was never conveyed to it. In these cases, not only will the expense of a probate be incurred, but the probate might result in a different distribution of assets than desired, particularly if a "pour-over" will did not exist to transfer omitted assets to the trust. Assets should be transferred to a trust immediately after the trust agreement is signed. But not all assets. Which assets should be owned by the trust, and which ones should be titled in some other manner? Here are the author's thoughts on that question.

REAL ESTATE.

Absent a specific reason to the contrary, major assets such as real property and investments should be owned by the trust, including real property in other states. If a trust has been chosen as the principal vehicle for the transfer of ownership after death, you want the major assets be owned by the trust. That way, transfer of the asset after your death will be governed by the terms of the trust agreement and probate will be avoided. Having assets in the trust will also give the successor trustee easy access to them for cost of care or emergencies in the event of incapacity.

Title to real property is transferred by deed, which must be acknowledged before a notary public and recorded. Although the wording of the deed will vary from one state to the next, a conveyance to a trust is normally made by a "bargain and sale" deed, quitclaim deed or similar type of deed which transfers "after-acquired" title but does not create any warranties by the trustor. It is important that the right to after-acquired title also be conveyed to the trust so that any interest that the trustor subsequently acquires will automatically flow through to the trust pursuant to the deed. For instance, if you are purchasing a home or other real property on an installment land contract, and the deed assigning the purchaser's interest in the contract to the trust did not carry "after-acquired" title with it under state law, the trust might not acquire full legal title when the contract was paid off, even though a deed from the vendor was received and recorded after all payments under the contract were made. This particular shortcoming could be remedied by legal action, but it would be far easier to use the proper words of conveyance in the original instrument.

But you should be aware that use of a quitclaim deed rather than

a warranty deed could result in the loss of title insurance coverage under the terms of many policies. Normally, a trustor will want to avoid
making the personal warranties which are contained in a warranty deed.
The quandary is that, under the policies issued in many states, he might
lose his title insurance coverage unless a warranty deed is used. Someone
concerned about the possibility of losing title insurance coverage should
consult with a knowledgeable attorney before conveying real property to
a trust. Whether or not this dilemma exists will depend on terms of the
title policy used in the particular jurisdiction where the real property is
situated.

ANNUITIES.

Although ownership of an annuity can be assigned to a revocable
living trust without income tax consequences, this is not commonly done.
Most people continue individual ownership, making certain that a power
of attorney exists giving someone, as agent, the authority to liquidate the
annuity if funds are needed and deposit them in the trust account.

A related question is whether to name individuals as direct beneficiaries or to name the trust. If the trust is named as beneficiary, the funds
would be exposed to expenses of last illness and creditor claims. If individuals are named as direct beneficiaries, the proceeds will not be subject
creditor claims under most circumstances. As long as a power of attorney
exists giving the agent authority to liquidate the annuity or transfer it to
the trust later if funds are needed, it seems preferable to leave ownership
of an annuity in the name of the trustor.

IRAs AND PENSION RIGHTS

One major exception to the general rule of transferring all major assets to the trust is individual retirement accounts, 401(k)s, 403(b)s and

similar tax-deferred investment accounts in the trustor's name. Tax-deferred accounts are, of necessity, titled in the name of the taxpayer; they cannot be transferred to a trust. A tax-deferred investment could be liquidated and the proceeds transferred to the trust, but not the retirement plan itself. However, liquidating and distributing would subject the funds to income taxation and defeat the plan's purpose as a tax-deferral vehicle. Since ownership of these investments can be passed by beneficiary designation and without probate, it would make no sense to cash them in and lose a portion to income taxation.

As a general rule, a trust should not even be named as beneficiary of an IRA, 401(k), 403(b) or the like. Assuming that you want your spouse to become the owner upon your death, he or she should be named as the primary beneficiary because tax laws afford a surviving spouse far greater flexibility and options for continued deferral of taxation than a trust. The options available to a trust to continue deferring are much more limited, basically only for five years after death. As a result, the spouse is commonly named as the primary beneficiary and the trust as contingent beneficiary in case the spouse dies at the same time or before the trustor.

STOCKS AND BONDS.

With the exception of IRAs, 401(k)s, 403(b)s and other tax-deferred accounts discussed above, investments should generally be re-titled in the name of your trust. If securities are owned individually at the time of death, a probate could be necessary. If owned jointly, they would go to the surviving joint owner(s) upon your death, which might differ from the plan of disposition set up in the trust.

Note that in this author's opinion it is better not to take physical possession of bearer bonds and stock certificates. There are numerous advantages in owning them in "street name;" i.e., with the brokerage firm taking possession of the certificate and giving you a monthly or quarterly statement. The advantages of street accounts outweigh the risks of taking possession of the certificates, in the author's opinion. If a stock certificate ever gets lost and needs to be sold, you, your conservator, your executor, or your successor trustee, as the case may be, will have to deal with the company's transfer agent. The transfer agent (usually a bank) is responsible for administering the corporation's stock ownership records. If a certificate has been lost, the transfer agent will require you or your successor in interest to sign an agreement to indemnify and hold the transfer agent harmless from loss in case the original certificate later shows up. The transfer agent will also insist on a bond, which will cost approximately 2% of value of the lost security.

I have known people who held many certificates in their own name rather than in a street account, apparently out of distrust of brokerage firms. They have no understanding of the burden they will be placing on a conservator, successor trustee or executor who will some day have to deal with dozens of transfer agents, each one wanting a certified copy of the death certificate, a copy of letters testamentary, affidavits and perhaps a certified copy of the will or trust agreement.

While caution is always healthy in the investment arena, the risks associated with owning securities in street name seem well down the list of investment concerns. The risk that a major brokerage firm might improperly pledge or commingle the securities it holds in street name with its own assets has always seemed remote to this author. Even assuming the worst, the account is insured against this risk by the Securities Investor Protection Corporation (SIPC), up to $500,000, including up to $100,000 cash. The Securities Investors Protection Corporation has not had financial problems like many of the other quasi-governmental agencies and is in good financial condition. In addition, most brokerage firms carry private insurance over and above the SIPC ceiling, and this insures customer accounts against custodial risks of this type into the millions of dollars per account. With the accounts being so well insured, the worst case scenario would seem to be one of delay in recovering more than ultimate loss.

In addition, owning securities in street name also provides a better paper trail for tax reporting, accounting for stock splits and dividends and valuation. All your successor in interest will have to do is look at your statements to see what the trust owned as opposed to looking for certificates and wondering whether every last one was found, whether there have been stock splits and the like.

BANK ACCOUNTS.

Major bank accounts should be re-titled in the name of the trust. However, most people like to maintain one joint account as a depository for Social Security and pension checks and for paying everyday living expenses. This avoids having to re-establish automatic payments and deposits of pension and Social Security checks. It also assures that some cash will be immediately available to the spouse or co-owner in the event of death or disability. If you are concerned about a simultaneous death, the trust could be named as a contingent beneficiary on the joint account by use of a "pay-on-death" rider (bank) or "transfer-on-death" rider (brokerage firm), which would eliminate any need for probate.

Certificates of deposit could also be retitled in the name of the trust. If the bank would impose an early withdrawal penalty, name the trust as beneficiary and make the change in title as they fall due. Re-titling will make it easier for your successor trustee if and when he or she has to take over.

MOTOR VEHICLES AND BOATS.

Vehicles can be owned by the trust or not, depending on the situation. Some people transfer ownership to the trust while others prefer to own their vehicles individually in the belief that it shields the trust assets from possible liability in the event of a fatal accident. A revocable living trust will not protect your assets from ordinary creditors during your lifetime; however, it might in the event of an at-fault accident in which the trustor died. This is a question of state law. The trust becomes a separate legal entity after death, and if the trustor became liable in his personal capacity for negligent driving, the trust assets might not be exposed to liability. This defense would only come into issue, of course, in the event of a judgment in excess of insurance coverage. Liability insurance is obviously still the most important consideration.

In most states at least one vehicle can be transferred through the state department of motor vehicles without probate. If additional vehicles needed to be transferred, a small estate affidavit procedure might be available to cover the second or third vehicle. There may also be the option of a beneficiary deed, discussed at page 48. As a result of these options, there probably is not a great risk of necessitating a probate by owning vehicles individually.

Title to airplanes can only be transferred through the Federal Aviation Agency in Oklahoma City, Oklahoma. Many people hold title to their aircraft in limited liability companies or corporations to insulate themselves from liability, in which case the stock or other ownership interest should be owned by the trust. But there is no reason these assets could not be titled directly in the name of the trustee.

TANGIBLE PERSONAL PROPERTY.

Title to household goods, furniture, furnishings, jewelry, antiques, coin collections, and other tangible personal property is normally transferred to the trust by a bill of sale or schedule attached to the declaration of trust or trust agreement. It should be made clear which items are to be owned by the trust and which are to remain in the trustor's individual name. And there should be no doubt as to who gets what items when you pass away or the trust terminates. The more specific your directions to your successor trustee, the more appreciative he or she will be.

PARTNERSHIPS AND MUTUAL FUNDS.

Some investors own limited partnership interests which they purchased through a brokerage firm. Even if your brokerage account is held in street name and the partnership interest is reflected on your monthly statement and priced at your original investment, it is owned by you personally and not by the brokerage firm in street name. It is not sufficient to merely re-title your brokerage account into the name of the trust. You have to go one step further and contact the general partner to find out what their requirements are for transferring the partnership interest to the trust.

The same consideration may apply to mutual funds. Except for IRAs, 401(k)s, 403(b)s and other retirement plans with account balances (of which the brokerage firm is the custodian), a brokerage firm might not hold title to a mutual fund in street-name. The brokerage firm might merely "network" it on your monthly statement as a convenience to you, with the mutual fund administrator being the primary record keeper and you the owner. If the brokerage firm does not contact the fund to change ownership to the trust, you should do so yourself. If this step is not taken, a probate might be needed some day.

PROMISSORY NOTES, TRUST DEEDS AND LAND SALE CONTRACTS.

Intangible assets of this nature should ordinarily be transferred to the trust in order to avoid probate. Again, you want disposition after your death to be governed by the terms of the trust agreement. You also want these assets to be readily accessible by your successor trustee in the event of incapacity. Intangible personal property, such as promissory notes, are transferred by an "assignment," which can be done either by a separate form of assignment or by an endorsement on the reverse side "Assigned to _____, Trustee of the _____ Trust, Under Agreement Dated xx/xx/xx," and signed by you as the payee.

A separate assignment is needed for trust deeds and other interests in real property; it should be acknowledged before a notary public and recorded to complete the transfer.

A revocable living trust must be "funded" by transferring assets to the trustee.

GOVERNMENT BONDS.

If you own government bonds, make application to the Bureau of Public Debt or the Federal Reserve Bank on Form PF 1851 to get them reissued in the name of the trust. The preferred manner of taking title is " John Doe, trustee of the John Doe Trust, U/A dated xx/xx/xx." "U/A," by the way, stands for "Under Agreement dated." It is a common abbreviation throughout the financial world.

LIFE INSURANCE.

A life insurance policy has three parties: the **owner**, who bought the policy. Unless an irrevocable payout election has been made with respect to the policy, the owner can cash the policy in, change beneficiaries, convert the cash value to an annuity, etc. The **insured** is the person whose life is being insured. The person insured can be someone other than the owner. The **beneficiary** is the person who gets the proceeds on death of the insured.

You may or may not want to name the trust as beneficiary of your life insurance policies. Yes, it would be convenient to have the policy proceeds distributed as provided in the trust agreement. However, naming the trust as beneficiary would expose the proceeds to creditors' claims, including costs of last illness. As a result of this disadvantage, many trustors name the spouse or children as primary beneficiary and name the trust as contingent beneficiary in case of simultaneous death.

You could transfer ownership of the policy to the trust if it furthered your objective. This would place the trustee in a position to cash the policy in, or to name the trust as beneficiary, or to change other incidents of ownership according to the authority given by the terms of the trust agreement.

If the trustor owns a policy on the life of someone else, ownership of the policy should be transferred to the trust. Otherwise, a probate might be required if the trustor died before the insured.

Contact the insurance company for their form to designate a new beneficiary or change ownership. The preferred nomenclature for naming a trust as beneficiary is "[name of successor trustee], or such successor trustee as may be hereafter named, as Trustee of _____ Living Trust, U/A dated xx/xx/xx."

CHAPTER EIGHT

A Trust or a Will?!

By now, it should be apparent that almost every estate planning decision involves trade-offs! There are advantages and disadvantages associated with almost any decision to be made, including the question of whether to opt for a will or for a living trust. With so many intangibles, it is impossible to make a general pronouncement that one is superior to the other. In some cases, the decision will be easy, and in others it will be a close call. The discussion that follows is an attempt to make the decision easier.

BENEFITS OF LIVING TRUSTS.

Let's assume that you have established a revocable living trust, by which is meant that you have signed a trust agreement and re-titled your major assets in your name as trustee of the trust. After your death or incapacity, a child, friend or financial institution is named in the trust agreement to serve as the successor trustee. Or your co-trustee will continue as sole trustee, as the case may be. Here are the major benefits of this arrangement.

1. Avoiding conservatorship. If your health fails and you become unable to manage your financial affairs, bills will still have to be paid, and assets may have to be sold to raise cash for cost of care. Without a trust, a conservatorship (known as "guardianship of the estate" in some states) might be the only answer. A conservatorship is a court-supervised proceeding in which a conservator (guardian of the estate) is appointed by the court, with notice and an opportunity to object being given to you as the person alleged to be incompetent. It involves attorney fees at the inception, attorney fees at the annual account and maybe attorney time in between. It is an expensive proceeding because it will probably continue for the rest of your life. In this author's opinion, a conservatorship is always to be avoided if you have a trustworthy friend or relative to take over in the event of incapacity. A conservatorship is potentially even more expensive than a probate because it involves attorney fees, court costs, annual bond fee, and ongoing court supervision. But with a trust, your successor trustee (or co-trustee) will be able to manage the income and assets free of court supervision. A trust is an excellent way to anticipate the possibility of incapacity, and this is one of the most important reasons to consider a trust. A durable power of attorney, also known as a "poor man's trust," might suffice, but it is not intended for long-term disability. For a long-term situation, nothing beats a living trust!

2. Avoiding probate. The second major advantage of a living trust is that it avoids the need for probate after your death. If you die without a trust, a probate would probably be necessary to settle final matters and transfer assets to your successors, at least as to "probate assets," as discussed on pages 16-19. The economics depend in large measure on the laws of the state where you live. In some states, such as New Jersey, the cost of probate is so minimal that it might cost more to set up and fund a trust than to do a probate. Living trusts will be relatively rare as probate-avoidance vehicles in states where cost of probate is minimal. But in states having high cost of probate, such as New York, Florida and California, living trusts are commonly chosen over wills. Many thousands of dollars of probate expense can be saved for your successors by establishing a trust.

The economics greatly favor trusts in the longer term. In most states the cost of probate will be higher than the cost of establishing and fund-

Economics greatly favor trusts in the longer term.

ing a living trust. The economics favor a trust even if you die the next month. But the cost savings get amplified over the years because the cost of probate keeps rising, whereas with a trust, you will have the legal expenses behind you, fixed in time. This is a relevant consideration because if a couple is retiring at age 65, it is statistically likely that one of them will live until almost 90. If legal fees rise by an average of 5% a year, it might cost three times as much to do a probate then as it would when a trust is being considered as an option. Using some very arbitrary assumptions, if it cost $1,000 to set up a trust and $3,000 to do a probate today, your heirs would be $2,000 ahead even if you died the next month. If you live for another 20 years, that probate might cost $9,000, in which case a trust would have saved your beneficiaries $8,000. A trust would save your beneficiaries an immense amount of money in the long run.

The one exception to the economics in favor of trusts is people with few assets or little liquidity. They might be better off to keep the extra cash it would take to go the trust route. My advice to people with little liquidity is to hang onto precious resources rather than trying to save probate expenses for the next generation. With the judicious use of joint ownership and beneficiary designations, people with small or modest estates can often arrange their affairs so that an inexpensive small estate affidavit might be the most that is needed after death. If a formal probate is needed, my advice is to let the next generation worry about it!

3. Avoiding Delay. Advocates of revocable living trusts like to emphasize the immediacy of distribution with a living trust compared with a will. The assumption is that distribution to the beneficiaries will be delayed with a probate proceeding, whereas a trustee will distribute right away. This assumption is not entirely accurate in either case. In situations where it is obvious from the outset that an estate has excess cash, the executor of a will can make a partial distribution almost immediately, the only difference being that, depending on the state in question, an executor might have to get approval of the probate court. Court approval would only be a formality.

You should also be aware that certain responsibilities always have to be fulfilled, regardless of whether a will or a trust is chosen. Many of these responsibilities are the same for a successor trustee as an executor: expenses of last illness have to be determined and paid, along with other creditors; and final tax returns must be filed. The home or stocks might have to be sold, in which case a fiduciary income tax return (Form 1041) would be required, even for a trust. This all takes time, and neither a trustee nor an executor will be able to close and distribute what remains until all creditors have been paid, all tax returns filed and all other responsibilities fulfilled. In short, there is no theoretical reason that a trust should result in faster closure than a will followed by probate.

Having said all of that, I must confess that there is probably some truth in the popular belief that probate results in delay. It has to do with the propensity of attorneys to procrastinate! Closing an estate is not the most exciting item on a busy attorney's to-do list. So an estate will often share the back burner with other less urgent matters. This can be very frustrating from the client's point of view. Not only is distribution delayed, but the longer an attorney's file is open, the higher the attorney fees will be.

4. Maintaining privacy. Trusts are promoted by some practitioners as a great way to keep matters private, and this appeals to some people. After a person's death, his or her will is filed in a probate proceeding and becomes a matter of public record, whereas a trust agreement is not normally filed with the court. To that extent, use of a will may entail some loss of privacy. But there is another way to look at the privacy consideration. Probate files have to be among the least scrutinized of all court files. When was the last time you went down to the courthouse, out of curiosity, to see how big an estate was, or who was getting what?! And bear in mind that the court file usually will not reveal the total size of the estate anyway because non-probate assets, such as life insurance, annuities, joint bank accounts and the like, are usually not included in the inventory which is filed with the court. If taxing authorities are the concern, rest assured that they have far better means of satisfying themselves as to the size of a deceased person's taxable estate than an asset list in a probate file.

Sometimes, however, privacy is an important consideration. If the decedent had owned and operated a business that the estate was trying to sell, you would not want the prospective buyer to know that the estate has a liquidity problem. The estate would be at a disadvantage in negotiations if a prospective buyer were able to examine the court file and learn what valuation the estate had used or that the estate needed cash to pay estate taxes, for example. The same applies to sale of a farm or ranch: nothing is ever to be gained by having a prospective buyer know of weaknesses in the seller's financial situation.

SOME BENEFITS OF PROBATE.

Everyone has heard horror stories about probate – endless delay, horrendous legal expense, etc. – so the immediate thought is, why not do a trust and avoid probate?! That might be fine in many situations, but probate is not always bad, even if you assume it costs more and involves delay. Under some circumstances, it can be advantageous to own assets individually so that probate will be required. Here are some situations where probate offers tangible benefits not available to living trusts.

1. Family allowance. Probate will often benefit the surviving family if the decedent's estate is insolvent. The surviving spouse and minor children typically have the right to petition the probate court for a "family allowance." If, for instance, the decedent's costs of last illness, medical expenses, credit card debt, state claims for reimbursement of welfare outlays, etc., exceeded the assets, the estate would be insolvent. Its liabilities exceed its assets. The pertinent question, when there are not enough assets to go around, is who gets paid first and who gets left out? The family allowance is given a very high position on the statutory schedule of priorities that applies when an estate is insolvent. The surviving spouse and/or minor children can petition the court for a monthly family allowance, which gets paid "off the top" for a period of time. Only what remains will be prorated among lower-priority claimants some months later when the estate is closed. The family allowance can be a very substantial benefit to the surviving family.

This special benefit for the immediate family would likely not be available in most states if the decedent's assets were owned by a living trust – all of the assets would be exposed to claims of the creditors.

2. Homestead award. Some states award a homestead allowance to the surviving spouse or children, and this takes precedence over the claims of general creditors. If the decedent did not own a home, the survivors might be entitled to a cash award in lieu of a homestead allowance. Either way, it would have a higher priority than general creditors and would be awarded to the survivors at the expense of creditors if there were not enough assets to go around. This is another example where the probate laws of many states favor wills and intestacy over trusts.

3. Unknown creditors. Creditors must present their claims within the claim period designated by the state's probate code — typically in the range of four to twelve months after publication of notice in the newspaper. If a creditor does not timely present its claim and the estate is closed, it will be barred, even if the creditor did not know about the death or realize that he or she had a claim! If, for example, the decedent had been involved in a high risk business as a sole proprietor, or if there is a potential for claims from unknown individuals (such as malpractice claims or products liability claims), those claims might be cut off at the end of the creditor claim period. (Of course, if the executor has actual knowledge about a creditor or potential claim, then specific notice would have to be given).

A living trust would avoid probate but would not cut off creditors' claims – creditors could have up to 6 years to pursue the assets owned by the trust and perhaps even to pursue the beneficiaries to whom trust assets had been distributed! In order to eliminate this difference between wills and trusts, a few states have passed legislation authorizing the trustee of a trust to publish notice to creditors and "cleanse" the assets of unknown claims.

4. Avoiding litigation. Many attorneys are of the opinion that a succession procedure which is court-supervised – i.e., probate – reduces the prospect of a dispute among the heirs or beneficiaries and increases the likelihood that the decedent's last wishes will be carried out. Other practitioners, primarily those who advocate for living trusts, believe that a pending lawsuit such as probate is an invitation to someone who is otherwise disposed to litigate. There is no way, of course, to prove or disprove either view point because everything is anecdotal, and you never know what the outcome would have been had the decedent opted for the other alternative. In this author's opinion, it depends more on the family dynamics than the vehicle for succession transfer. Situations with surviving spouses and stepchildren and situations with dysfunctional families have the highest prospect of litigation. It is just as easy to litigate issues about undue influence or mental incapacity with respect to a trust as it is a will!

THE COST OF PROBATE.

Since the subject of probate itself is not well understood, there is misunderstanding as to the cost of probate. After someone passes away, certain responsibilities have to be fulfilled: filing final tax returns, paying creditors, selling assets, etc. Some will most likely be done by an attorney, some by the executor or successor trustee, and some by other professionals. Someone interested in estimating the cost of probate should distinguish between the "hard cost" of probate and separate out the general responsibilities that even a successor trustee would have to complete, such as tax return preparation, appraisal fees, and selling costs.

The hard costs of probate will include filing fees paid to the court, legal fees to an attorney or law firm, publication costs to a newspaper, possibly an executor's fee, and possibly fees to a court-appointed appraiser. These expenses will vary in significance from one estate to the next, but legal fees and executor fees will be the two largest items.

Almost every estate planning decision involves tradeoffs.

Executor's fee. An executor is entitled to be compensated for administering the estate. The amount is commonly set by the state probate code as a sliding-scale percentage of the gross value of the assets. The percentage is higher in some states than in others, of course. A smaller percentage might also be applied to some of the non-probate assets, such as jointly owned property, even though such assets are not subject to probate, at least if an estate or inheritance tax return has to be filed. Depending on the state, the executor's fee can be a significant expense, sometimes exceeding legal fees.

However, an executor can – and often does – waive the fee, in which case it will not be paid. Here's why. In the case of estates not large enough to owe estate, inheritance or income taxes and where the executor is also the sole beneficiary, he or she should waive the fee. That's because the fee would be taxable income to the executor, whereas the inheritance itself is not subject to income tax. It would make no sense to be paid a fee and have to pay income tax on it – better to take the entire inheritance with no income tax liability. Even where there are siblings or other beneficiaries who will share in the estate, executors will often waive the fee rather than charge their friends, siblings or other relatives and be taxed on it as well.

If an estate has taxes payable, a sole beneficiary-executor might consider taking an executor's fee. If the estate has substantial taxable income and the executor is in a lower income tax bracket, it might pencil out better to pay an executor's fee, have the executor pay additional income tax on it at his or her lower rate and thereby reduce the overall tax bill. For federal income tax purposes, an estate is only entitled to a $600 exclusion, and it does not get either a personal exemption or a standard deduction. The rates applicable to estates and trusts are steep, reaching the 35% bracket with taxable income of only $9,350 (2004 figure). See rate table on page 94. As a result, if the estate has taxable income and the executor is in a low bracket, overall taxes can sometimes be lowered by shifting income to the executor to give the estate a deduction. In the end, each situation has to be individually evaluated.

Legal fees. The other major component of probate is legal fees. Estimating legal fees is particularly difficult because there are numerous variables. Not only do hourly rates vary considerably from one region to another, they vary from one attorney or one law firm to the next. Even if the hourly rates of two attorneys are identical, one will probably get the task done more expediently than the other. Unfortunately, there is no way to quantify these unknowns.

In addition, what is a simple probate in one state can be quite complicated across a state line. It is tempting to criticize the states that have more complicated and, hence, more expensive, probate procedures. But bear in mind that those procedures provide additional protections for creditors, beneficiaries, and heirs at law who have something at stake.

My advice to someone needing an attorney to handle a probate is to have an initial conference with two or three and pick the one you feel most comfortable with, particularly if someone recommended him or her. Since they know what is involved in a basic probate, some attorneys will agree to handle a probate for a flat fee plus costs, such as court costs and publication expense. But the attorney will not know whether the executor will be diligent or whether a lot of extra work might end up being done in the attorney's office. Nor does the attorney what might crop up unexpectedly. So expect any flat fee agreement to cover only the most basic and carefully-defined legal responsibilities. Additional legal services above the basics will invariably be based on hourly rates.

In some states legal fees are commonly a percentage of the gross estate. Again, expect the fee agreement to cover only basic responsibilities with additional services, such as preparation of tax returns, at hourly rates. Even in states where attorney fees are scheduled by statute, there is nothing to preclude the attorney and executor from entering into an hourly agreement. They could also agree to do it for less than the percentage, but it is typically difficult to negotiate a lower percentage or flat fee.

Some attorneys prepare income and estate tax returns, and some do not. If you have a Certified Public Accountant or Enrolled Agent doing the tax returns, it might cost less.

CHAPTER NINE

ADMINISTRATION OF TRUSTS AND ESTATES

It is absolutely essential that the assets of any trust or estate that you are handling be kept separate from your personal assets. If trust or estate property becomes commingled, any doubt as to who owns what could be resolved against you as the fiduciary. It is conceivable that could become personally liable to the trust or estate.

Trust assets should be segregated even if it is your own revocable trust, and segregation is particularly critical if you are the fiduciary of someone else's trust or estate. The corollary is that good records should be kept. Fiduciaries who are computer literate should consider using Quick

Books or some other simple software program for the checking account. It will save time and expense in the long run.

REVOCABLE LIVING TRUSTS.

After a revocable living trust is set up, the assets and investments should be re-titled into the name of "John Smith, Trustee of the John Smith Revocable Living Trust dated XXXX." Trust books and records should be established and the cost basis for each asset memorialized. This information is readily available to you, the grantor, but it might be difficult information for the successor trustee to find many years down the road. Make it as easy as possible for your successor trustee. An accountant or tax return preparer can help determine your tax basis for capital gains tax purposes.

In tax parlance, a revocable living trust is known as a "grantor trust." John Smith, the trustor or "grantor," retained some interest in the trust assets, as a result of which the trust will not be treated as a separate legal entity for either income tax or estate tax purposes. In the case of a revocable living trust, that interest, or "string," is the right to amend or revoke the trust or receive money from the trust. Consequently, as long as John Smith, the trustor, is also the trustee or a co-trustee, the bank or brokerage firm will carry the account under John Smith's Social Security number and issue the 1099's at year end under John Smith's personal name and Social Security number. The trust will have no effect on Smith's taxable income or the way it is reported to the IRS. It would be the same if Smith resigns or becomes incapacitated, except that the successor trustee would be making the investment decisions and be responsible for signing the tax returns.

But if John Smith were to die, the trust will ordinarily become irrevocable. The successor trustee would assume control and would be required to submit Form SS-4 to the IRS to get an Employer Identification Number

(EIN) for the trust. The bank and brokerage firm will re-title the accounts in the successor trustee's name as "Trustee of the John Smith Revocable Living Trust dated XXXX." The 1099s at year end would be issued under the trust's new EIN. The significance of this difference is that the successor trustee will have to file an informational tax return (Form 1041) with the IRS by April 15th.

Note that if John and Mary Smith had been co-trustors and co-trustees and if Mary Smith continued as trustee after John Smith's death, the trust continuing to be revocable, an Employer Identification Number would not be required. Investment activity would be reported under Mary Smith's Social Security number (assuming she was the beneficiary).

ESTATES.

Unlike a revocable trust, an estate is treated as a separate legal entity for federal income tax purposes. If someone died on July 15, 2004, and had a will (or died intestate), the decedent's executor, after being appointed by the court, would apply to the IRS for an Employer Identification Number. The estate's tax year would end on June 30, 2005, the end of the eleventh calendar month after date of death. If the estate had income in excess of $600 (or a beneficiary who is a nonresident alien), the estate will be obligated to file a fiduciary tax return (Form 1041) by the 15th of the fourth month following the tax year end; i.e., by October 15, 2005, in this example.

An estate is taxed quite differently than individual taxpayers in several respects. Its income is determined in much the same manner as it would have been if received by the decedent; i.e., income is characterized as interest, dividends, capital gain, return of capital. And the estate gets to deduct its business expenses, taxes, investment expenses exceeding 2% of adjusted gross income, etc. But there are some major differences:

- Not being an individual, an estate does not get either a standard deduction or a personal exemption. The first $600 of taxable income is excluded and the rest gets taxed under the schedule in Example 11 below.

- The good news is that the estate gets to deduct distributions to its heirs and beneficiaries (limited, of course, by the amount of its taxable income). The distributions "pass through" to the beneficiary and are included on his or her personal income tax return.

EXAMPLE 11.

Income taxation of estate - The decedent passed away on July 15, 2004. The estate had taxable income of $10,000 and paid deductible expenses, such as legal fees, court costs, tax return preparation, etc., of $5,000 during the period ending June 30, 2005. No distributions were made to the two beneficiaries. The executor is obligated to file a From 1041 by October 15, 2005, using the estate's EIN. The taxable income of the estate would be $4,400 ($10,000 - $5,000 - $600). Income tax of $910 would be due under the following progressive tax rate schedule applicable to estates and non-grantor trusts.

From	To	Rate
$ 0	$1,900	15%
1,900	4,500	25%
4,500	6,850	28%
6,850	9,350	33%
9,350	++	35%

EXAMPLE 12.

Deduction for distributions - In the preceding example, if the estate had made a distribution of $4,400 or more to its beneficiaries, the estate could deduct the distribution and have no taxable income. It would owe no income tax. (The distribution would have to be made within 65 days of the estate's year end; i.e., by September 3, 2005).

However, each beneficiary would have $2,200 of additional taxable income to account for on his or her personal Form 1040 income tax return due by April 15, 2006. The beneficiaries, as well as the Internal Revenue Service, would be informed of the distributions through the Schedule K-1 (part of the 1041 fiduciary return). If the beneficiaries are in a very high income tax bracket, they might prefer to let the estate pay in this simple example. But with larger taxable amounts, the incentive will ordinarily be to distribute because the beneficiaries will be in a lower bracket than the estate. A trust or estate reaches the 35% bracket with taxable income of $9,350. By comparison, an unmarried individual taxpayer does not reach the 35% bracket until his or her taxable income reaches $311,950! With such highly-compressed brackets, it generally is not advisable to allow taxable income to accumulate in an estate or irrevocable trust – it should be distributed so that the estate will get a deduction.

Normally, taxable income in an estate or non-grantor trust is undesirable because the tax brackets are so compressed and the rate rises so quickly. If the estate had taxable income of $44,000 rather than $4,400, it would owe income taxes of $15,000! Unless the beneficiaries were also in the 35% bracket, the estate would want to distribute the taxable income so the beneficiaries would be taxed on it at their lower rate.

TRUSTS.

Non-grantor trusts are treated the same as estates, with the following minor exceptions:

- Only $300 of taxable income is excluded, as opposed to $600 for an estate.

- A trust must file an income tax return if it has any taxable income, even if the amount is less than $300. It also must file if it has gross income in excess of $600, even if it has no taxable income, and it must file if any of the beneficiaries is a non-resident alien, regardless of the amount of gross or taxable income.

- The trust's tax year must end on December 31st, and the tax return (Form 1041) will be due on April 15th.

PART IV

....

Taxable Estates

CHAPTER TEN

Gift, Estate and Inheritance Taxes

An estimated two per cent of all estates were taxable for federal estate tax purposes when the exemption was $600,000. That percentage is lower now that the exemption has increased to $1.5 million, and the percentage will continue to decline as the exemption continues to rise. If your estate, or the combined estates of you and your spouse, exceed the exemption, you should have a basic understanding of how the combined gift-estate tax works.

The tax is highly confiscatory, starting at 45% (2004 rates) on the first dollar over the exemption. All legitimate means should be taken to minimize the tax or avoid it entirely.

On the other hand, if the combined estates of you and your spouse are well below the exemption, and you do not expect to inherit any significant amount or win the lottery, you might want to skip this chapter. Keep in mind, however, that in adding up the value of your estates, virtually everything must be included – proceeds of life insurance policies, living trust assets, joint accounts, and even the actuarial value of your spouse's survivorship rights, if any, under your pension or annuity.

For many years the federal estate tax exemption was $600,000. In 1997, Congress passed legislation that raised it in steps over several years to $1 million. In 2001, Congress passed new legislation that increased the exemption faster and higher. That law also created different exemption amounts for the estate tax and the gift tax. Here is a summary of the law as it now stands:

| | | Gift Tax | |
Year	Estate Exemption	Highest Rate	Exemption Amount
2004	$1.5 million	48%	$1 million
2005	$1.5 million	47%	$1 million
2006	$2 million	46%	$1 million
2007	$2 million	45%	$1 million
2008	$2 million	45%	$1 million
2009	$3.5 million	45%	$1 million
2010	Estate/GST repealed	0	$1 million
2011	$1 million	55%	$1 million

One quirk in this legislation is that it sunsets after the year 2010, meaning that if Congress takes no further action in the meantime, the tax law applicable to gifts and estates after the year 2010 will revert to the law as it existed in the year 2001– an exemption of $1 million for both gifts and estates occurring in 2011 and thereafter. (Although the gift tax rate will be a flat 35% on amounts over the $1 million exemption).

People with non-taxable estates should understand that they (actually their heirs or beneficiaries) may have an interest in the reforms. It might seem that elimination of the estate tax would not affect someone who does not have a taxable estate. However, the proposals always include provisions to eliminate the step-up-in-basis rules and replace them with complicated "carry-over" basis rules. Appreciated assets of a decedent now receive a step-up in basis to the date-of-death market value, which essentially eliminates the built-in capital gain tax for the heirs. Upon repeal of the estate tax, the stepped-up basis rules would be replaced with new and complicated "carry-over" basis rules, which could subject the heirs to capital gains tax, even if the estate was not taxable.

EXAMPLE 13.

Stepped-up basis vs. carryover basis - Assume that Congress does not change the estate-gift tax law as it now stands and that Maximillian dies in 2010 possessed of a large estate, including some stock that he purchased decades ago for $10 per share. After splits, it was worth the equivalent of $500 per share at the time of his death. The law excludes $1.3 million from the carry-over basis, but his estate is well in excess of that amount and does not qualify for a step-up in basis. His estate or heirs will pay capital gains tax on the $490 per share increase in value when it is sold.

If the estate tax had been in effect, there might have been estate tax on the value of the stock, had his estate been large enough, but the $490 increase in value would have totally escaped income taxation. Either the estate or his heirs could sell it for $500 and pay no capital gains tax.

HOW THE COMBINED FEDERAL ESTATE/GIFT TAX WORKS.

The "estate tax" is actually a unified gift and estate tax, meaning that essentially the same tax structure applies to both lifetime gifts and to the taxable estate remaining at the time of death. A person cannot give away a large estate and expect to avoid estate taxes – lifetime taxable gifts are lumped together with the net taxable estate remaining at death and treated as one. The estate gets a credit on its estate tax return for any gift taxes previously paid.

EXAMPLE 14.

Effect of gifts on lifetime exemption - Frank has a large estate and knows it will be subject to the estate tax on his death. Shortly before his death and wanting to reduce the estate tax bill, Frank made a gift of $100,000 cash to his daughter, Susie. Since the amount of the gift exceeded the annual gift tax exclusion ($11,000 in 2004 - discussed immediately following), a taxable gift of $89,000 was made. Frank (or his executor) will be required to file a gift tax return (Form 709) by April 15 of the next calendar year. This taxable gift follows Frank to his grave and has the effect of reducing his lifetime estate tax exemption by $89,000 (or of raising his taxable estate by $89,000, depending on how you want to view it). Taxable gifts are brought back into the estate on the estate tax return (Form 706), and credit is given for any gifts taxes actually paid.

If Frank passed away in 2004 or 2005, his estate's exemption would be $1,411,000 ($1,500,000 minus $89,000).

It should be noted that unlimited gifts can be made to one's spouse – the unlimited marital deduction for transfers to spouses applies to both lifetime gifts and to transfers after death.

ANNUAL GIFT TAX EXCLUSION.

For many years the annual gift tax exclusion was $10,000. It is now indexed to inflation and is currently $11,000. Up to $11,000 per year per donee can be given away each year without using any of one's lifetime exemption or having to file a gift tax return. The annual exclusion applies to as many people as you make gifts to! You could make total gifts of $11,000 to each child, cousin, aunt, uncle and stranger each year, year after year, and not use any of your lifetime exemption ($1.5 million in 2004 and 2005). Your spouse could do the same, so that $22,000 could be gifted each year to each donee. If the couple also wanted to include the donee's spouse, up to $44,000 could be gifted to the child and spouse — Mother gives $11,000 each to child and spouse; Father does the same. Their lifetime exemptions are not reduced.

EXAMPLE 15.

Annual gift tax exclusion - If, in Example 14, Frank had given $50,000 to Susie and $50,000 to her husband, he would be entitled to two annual exclusions of $11,000 each, or $22,000. He would only use up only $78,000 of his lifetime exemption for estate tax purposes as a result of the $100,000 gift rather than $89,000. If this was his first taxable gift, his remaining exemption would drop to $1,422,000 if he passed away in 2004 or 2005 ($1,500,000 minus $78,000).

EXAMPLE 16.

Maximum lifetime gift tax exemption - One inconsistency has arisen as a result of the tax reforms enacted in 2001. Whereas the exemption for federal estate tax purposes is $1.5 million in the year 2004 and is scheduled to rise in later years, the gift tax exemption is only $1 million and remains constant. For example, let's assume that Bill gives $1,500,000 to his daughter. This is his first gift. A Form 709 gift tax return will be due by April 15th of the following calendar year. The annual exclusion of $11,000 and lifetime exemption of $1 million will both apply. There will be a taxable gift of $489,000, and gift taxes starting at the rate of 41% will be due. In this case it might have been better to gift only $1 million and keep all of his lifetime exemption for use by his estate.

DO YOU HAVE A POTENTIAL ESTATE TAX PROBLEM?

You do not have an estate tax problem unless your net taxable estate (i.e., after debt and costs of administration) exceeds the exemption. But this is determined at the time of death, not now. By steadily raising the exemption and then letting it revert to $1 million after 2010, the 2001 legislation has added a great deal of uncertainty to estate planning. Fluctuations in value and consumption have always been unknowns. But for the next several years, changes in the exemption level and possible future legislation are also big factors.

Determining the size of an unmarried person's estate is a straightforward matter of adding up the fair market values of everything owned and deducting mortgages, debts, and estimated costs of administration. If your net estate is less than $1,500,000 (2004-2005 figure) and you do not expect a significant increase, as through inheritance, then your estate will not be subject to the estate tax, at least if you die before Congress changes the law. Again, be sure to include the proceeds of your life insurance policies, annuity balances, IRAs, living trust assets, jointly-owned assets and other "non-probate" assets. The "taxable estate" includes not only the assets you own but also any in which you retained an interest.

EXAMPLE 17.

Effect of retained interests - Trevor, who is single, has an estate of $2 million, not including his home, which he gave to his son two years before his death. The home was worth $500,000 at that time, and he retained a life estate because he wanted to continue living in it. Under state law, his sons will own the home outright upon Trevor's death without probate. However, under estate tax law, the entire fair market value of the home will be included in Trevor's gross taxable estate upon his death due to the retained interest, his life estate. If the home appreciated in value between the time of the gift and the date of Trevor's death, the higher figure will have to be used.

Married couples have to consider what their combined estates are worth, who owns what, and how much will pass to the surviving spouse. What is the total value of all assets owned by either or both spouses, again including life insurance, IRA's, living trust, annuities, jointly-owned property, stocks, bonds, real estate? You also have to include the actuarial value of your spouse's survivor's benefits under an annuity or pension if a joint-and-several payout election was made. If the combined total exceeds $1,500,000 (2004-2005 figure), after deducting debt, then the couple might have a federal estate tax problem. But probably not on the first death. The tax problem normally does not arise until the death of the second spouse. Here's why.

As a result of the unlimited marital deduction, the first spouse to die can leave an unlimited amount to the surviving spouse, free of federal estate taxes. This is true even if the person had no will or trust at all! To the extent that assets pass to the surviving spouse, the deceased spouse's estate will be entitled to a marital deduction on its estate tax return. Since the marital deduction is unlimited in amount, someone with a $50 million estate could leave it all to his or her spouse, and no estate tax would have to be paid. It even includes situations where there was no will or living trust – i.e., where the spouse as an heir at law.

The tax problem arises when the surviving spouse passes away. The second estate gets the same lifetime exemption, $1.5 million (2004-2005 figure). And the tax rate still starts at 45% (2004 rate) on the first dollar exceeding $1,500,000. However, if the entire estate of the first spouse to die passes to the surviving spouse, all of the assets will now be bunched up in the estate of the surviving spouse. The second estate will be up to $1,500,000 larger (ignoring inflation, change in value, etc.) than it would be if the first estate had established a credit shelter trust (also called "by-pass trust") to utilize an exemption for each spouse. Estate tax will be levied at a minimum rate of 45% (2004 rate) on amounts exceeding the $1.5 million exemption.

DISCLAIMING.

Aside from fluctuations in value, possible inheritances should be considered in estimating the value of your estate. If you inherit from a friend or relative prior to passing away, the size of your estate will increase. If your estate already exceeds the exemption and you do not want an inheritance, you might want to disclaim it. Disclaiming is basically a legal way to refuse to accept an inheritance. If done properly, a disclaimer will not consume any of your remaining exemption. But be sure to do so immediately because if you accept benefits, the disclaimer might not be qualified; i.e., after accepting benefits, you could still reject the inheritance, but it would be treated as a taxable gift and reduce your federal estate tax exemption. Disclaiming requires prompt action and competent tax advice.

HOW A CREDIT SHELTER TRUST WORKS.

The key to estate planning for a couple with combined estates in excess of the exemption is the credit shelter trust, also known as a bypass trust. By using a credit shelter trust, a married couple can take advantage of two exemptions (one for each spouse) and significantly reduce federal estate tax liability and possibly eliminate it altogether. The will or living trust of the first spouse to die puts the full $1,500,000 exemption amount (2004-2005 figure) into a credit shelter trust rather than leaving the entire estate outright to the surviving spouse. The surviving spouse gets all the income from the credit shelter trust plus the right to invade the principal for his or her "health, education, maintenance and support." The surviving spouse can also be given a non-cumulative right to withdraw the greater of $5,000 or 5% of the principal each year. The trust is a separate legal entity, and its assets will not be included in the surviving spouse's taxable estate, even though he or she had a life estate in the income and a limited right to invade principal! The trust assets never belong to the surviving spouse having only a life estate, and the life estate ceases upon the death of the surviving spouse. As a result, the size of the surviving spouse's estate is kept correspondingly smaller. The children or other beneficiaries receive up to $3 million (2004-2005 figure) with no federal estate tax liability.

A credit shelter trust is the most basic estate planning strategy available to a married couple. A credit shelter trust can be set up after death via trust provisions in your will – after the estate has been administered and is ready to close, your executor will distribute the designated amount

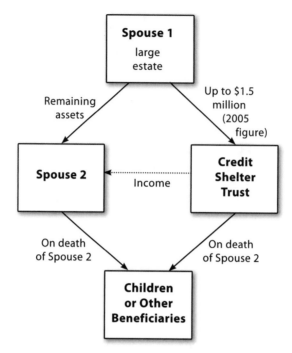

How a Credit Shelter Trust Works

from the estate to the trustee of the credit shelter trust. The other way is to set up (and fund, of course!) a revocable living trust which on your death distributes the designated amount to a credit shelter trust, all as provided for in the trust agreement. It makes no difference for estate tax purposes which way it is done as long as the proper tax provisions have been incorporated into the will or trust agreement. The estate tax savings are the same either way. But one or the other must be done before the first spouse passes away – the strategy is conceptually not available after one spouse passes away.

STATE INHERITANCE TAXES.

Approximately three fourths of the states have adopted what is commonly known as a "pick up" tax. This is not an additional inheritance tax on top of the federal estate tax. The federal estate tax law authorizes a credit on the Form 706 estate tax return (up to a certain maximum) for inheritance taxes paid to states due to the death of the decedent. Federal estate taxes payable to the IRS are reduced, dollar-for dollar, by the amount paid to the state, up to the allowable maximum. The overall tax liability is the same as though the state had no tax.

However, as a result of the 2001 legislation, the state tax credit allowed by federal law is being phased out. The maximum credit was lowered to 75% for deaths occurring in 2002, 50% for deaths in 2003, and 25% for deaths in 2004. The state tax credit disappears entirely after 2004 and is replaced by a deduction on the estate tax return. Reduction and elimination of the federal estate tax credit is causing a major loss of revenue for states with pick up taxes, and many are changing in their inheritance tax laws to compensate for the loss of revenue.

Some states have an inheritance tax rather than a "pick up" tax. Although an inheritance tax can take a variety of forms, inheritance tax structures typically grant an exemption of some amount and impose an inheritance tax on the balance going to the recipient. The exemptions are largest for the surviving spouse, less for children and even less for more distantly-related takers.

WHEN THE FEDERAL ESTATE TAX IS DUE.

The federal estate tax is due and payable nine months after date of death. If the estate tax return cannot be filed within nine months, due to events beyond the executor's control, such as delays in getting appraisals, an extension can be obtained. However, the estimated tax still must be paid within nine months or else interest and penalties will be incurred. If it turns out that too little estimated tax was paid in, interest and penalties will apply. As a result, it is important that valuation of assets be started as shortly after death as possible.

Farms and certain closely-held businesses get special consideration. An estate that is comprised almost entirely of a business, ranch or farm and meeting a very narrow definition can opt to pay in installments over as long as 14 years. However, even if your estate met the rigid qualifications, there are so many strings attached – plus complicated recapture provisions for the following ten years – that the exception is almost never used. So make your plans on the assumption that taxes will be due at the end of nine months.

LIFE INSURANCE TO PAY ESTATE TAXES.

It is important that the amount of estate taxes be anticipated so that sufficient liquidity will exist to pay them within the nine months allowed. For some people, liquidity will not be a problem because they own certificates of deposit, stocks, and bonds that can be sold. The securities enjoy a step-up in basis on death, so the estate can sell them with little or no income tax consequence. However, if liquid assets do not exist, a liquidity problem could exist. This is most often seen in estates where the bulk of the estate consists of a small business, ranch or farm. Unless the liquidity problem was anticipated, assets might have to be sold to raise cash to pay death taxes. Under these circumstances, life insurance should be considered as a source of liquidity for estate taxes.

For married couples, survivorship life insurance, or last-to-die insurance, as it is also called, is often used to provide liquidity for the estate taxes which will be due after the death of the second spouse. The policy insures the lives of both spouses and pays when the second spouse dies. These policies make sense because there usually is no estate tax due on the first death, due to the unlimited marital deduction. Because two lives are insured and the insurance company will not have to pay until the second death, the premiums are lower on these policies.

Who should own the policy. Note that if the decedent owned the policy, the size of his or her taxable estate will be increased by the amount of proceeds! That's not a good idea because, again, the minimum estate tax rate in 2004 is 45%. If someone has an estate of $2.5 million at death plus a $500,000 life insurance policy and dies owning the policy, the estate suddenly jumps to $3 million. Close to half of the policy proceeds will go to pay additional estate taxes!

Two strategies are commonly used to keep the policy proceeds out of the taxable estate and avoid paying more estate taxes. One is to have the policy owned directly by the children. The other is to have it owned by an irrevocable life insurance trust, or "ILIT." Either way, the proceeds will not be included in the taxable estate of the insured.

Ownership by children. If your entire estate will some day be transferred to an only child and the child is financially responsible, the simplest way to keep the policy proceeds from being included in your taxable estate and increasing the estate tax liability is to have your child purchase and own the policy. As long as you never owned the policy or held any

Federal estate taxes are highly confiscatory for large estates.

"strings" to it, the policy proceeds will not be included in your taxable estate. Your child applies for and purchases a policy on the lives of both parents and pays all the premiums. You can make a gift to the child each year of $11,000 (2004 figure) without using any of your $1,500,000 lifetime exemption ($22,000 if your spouse consents to gift splitting). The child will presumably use the gift money to pay the premium.

One risk in this arrangement, of course, is the financial responsibility of the child. Will your child use the gift money to pay the premium? If it is to be a gift, you can have no control over the use of the annual gift money. It has to be an unrestricted gift – i.e., no understandings or strings attached. If your child is financially irresponsible, the money might be used to buy a new car or a trip to Las Vegas. In addition, if the child suffers financial setbacks and is forced to declare bankruptcy, the policy itself would be an asset of his or her bankruptcy estate; the trustee in bankruptcy could use the cash surrender value to pay creditors. Or, if your child got divorced, the policy might be treated as a marital asset of which his or her spouse could claim a portion. If these possibilities concern you, you should consider using an irrevocable life insurance trust, discussed in the next section.

Note that several children could be made co-owners of a policy, but the problems and risks described in the preceding paragraph would be amplified if you did. The risk would be greater that one of them might decide to pocket the annual gift rather than paying the policy premium. There is also the risk that after your death one of them might not use his share of the policy proceeds to pay estate and inheritance taxes. Clearly, the purpose of the arrangement should always be well understood by the children, and you should feel confident that the proceeds and premium money will be used as intended. If not, consider use of an irrevocable life insurance trust.

Ownership by an irrevocable life insurance trust. An irrevocable life insurance trust (ILIT) is an irrevocable trust which owns a life insurance policy. Cash gifts are usually made to the trust annually to provide the trust with cash to pay the premium. Gifts to a trust do not normally qualify for the annual gift tax exclusion ($11,000 per donee in 2004) because the trust is not an individual. In order to qualify for the annual gift tax exclusion, the ILIT trust agreement must be drafted to include "Crummey" powers (named after a tax case). Your children, as beneficiaries of the trust, are given written notice of the contribution to the trust and a meaningful opportunity to withdraw it – at least three weeks. The children receive notice of the contribution but, knowing the purpose of the arrangement, let the time period pass. The trustee is then free to use gift money to pay the premium. A gift is deemed to have been made directly to the individuals since they could have withdrawn the funds, and it qualifies for the annual gift tax exclusion. Without Crummey powers, the gift to the trust could still be made, but it would not qualify for the annual exclusion and the donor's lifetime exemption would drop by the amount of the gift – to $1,489,000 in the first year, $1,478,000 in the second year, etc. (assuming $11,000 gifts in 2004 and 2005).

It is critical that the ILIT be set up properly and that notices to the beneficiaries be documented and handled with meticulous care. A responsible third party, such as a bank or trust company, should serve as trustee, give the notices, etc.

The same concepts can be used by an unmarried individual to purchase life insurance for estate tax liquidity and to keep the policy proceeds out of his or her estate. The policy, of course, would insure one life rather than two.

CHAPTER ELEVEN

CHARITABLE GIVING

One need not have a taxable estate or high income to get satisfaction from making charitable gifts; but, as this chapter will show, it certainly reduces the real cost if you do.

There can be both income tax and gift-estate tax benefits associated with charitable gifts. If you give $1,000 to your church or favorite charity and itemize deductions on your income tax return, you get a charitable deduction of $1,000. If you are in the 28% bracket, your income tax bill goes down by $280. If you passed away in possession of a taxable estate (more than $1.5 million in 2004 and 2005), the size of your estate will be $1,000 less than it would otherwise have been, and the federal estate tax bill would be $450 less. The point is that if you make a gift by will or trust after your death, your estate will get an estate tax deduction. But you will not get an income tax deduction as you would for a lifetime gift.

The tax law pertaining to charitable giving is actually very complex. It is a specialty that most attorneys, including this author, choose not to dabble in – unless you are intimately familiar with the subject, an error could easily deprive the client of the tax benefits upon which a gift was premised. One of the reasons for the complexity is "split interests." Rather than making an outright gift, many donors want to retain an interest in the gifted asset, such as the income for life, and let the remainder go to the charity upon death. The income interest has to be valued separately. This income interest reduces the value of the gift and the corresponding charitable deduction. In addition, there are different income tax consequences associated with giving appreciated land, appreciated stock, a tax-deferred account, and an installment land contract, to name a few that are often considered as charitable gifts.

Split interests will be discussed in some detail in this chapter, but the reader should be mindful of the fact that this chapter is intended only to explain the very basics of charitable giving. It is not intended to be a manual for making decisions with respect to gifts. You need a competent tax advice before making a sizeable gift.

INCOME TAXATION.

One of the immediate tax benefits is the itemized deduction for a gift to a qualified charitable organization. However, there is a limit on the amount that can be deducted each year. If the full deduction cannot be used in one year, the balance can be carried forward for up to five years and used on future tax returns.

EXAMPLE 18.

Limitation on income tax deduction - Andrew and Bonnie both have taxable estates. Their adjusted gross income is $150,000 per year. They give $100,000 cash to a charitable foundation. They get a deduction on their individual tax return the following April 15th. However, for cash gifts the deduction is limited to 50% of their adjusted gross income. They receive a deduction of $75,000 (half of $150,000) in the first year. They can carry the unused $25,000 forward and deduct it in the next tax year (subject, of course, to the same 50% limitation).

EXAMPLE 19.
Limitation on income tax deduction - Let's assume that rather than cash, Andrew and Bonnie give appreciated stock worth $100,000 to their favorite charity. They paid $10,000 for the stock many years ago, and the $90,000 gain would be subject to capital gains tax if they sold it. The charity, being a not-for-profit organization, can sell the stock and will pay no capital gains or income tax on the sale. As in the case of cash, Andrew and Bonnie get to deduct the contribution on their individual income tax return. But in the case of non-cash gifts, the annual deduction is limited to 30% of their adjusted gross income. With adjusted gross income of $150,000, their deduc-

The tax law pertaining to charitable giving is very complex.

tion is limited to $45,000 under these assumed facts. They deduct another $45,000 in the following year (or whatever 30% amounts to) and the balance in the third year. It would be the same result if they had donated appreciated land rather than stock. The charity could sell with no income tax consequences, and the donors could deduct the market value of the contribution without being taxed on the built-in capital gain. But always subject to the 30% limit in the case of non-cash gifts.

In all of these examples, of course, their estates, for federal estate tax purposes, will be $100,000 lower because they succeeded in removing $100,000 from their taxable estates.

Note that if the stock or land had depreciated in value, they would sell it, use the loss on their income tax returns and give cash to the charity.

EXAMPLE 20.

Retained use - Assume that Andrew and Bonnie gave their home to the charity on the condition that they could continue to live in it until they were both deceased. It gets complicated now because, they have retained a life estate. The value of the life estate is determined under Treasury Regulations based on their ages and the applicable federal interest rate in effect at the time. They get an income tax deduction for the value of the gift, which is the fair market value of the home less the value of the retained life estate. Again, the deduction is subject to the annual limit of 30% of adjusted gross income.

However, since they retained a life estate, the entire value of the home will be included in their taxable estates for federal estate tax purpose! They got an income tax deduction for part of the value, but their estates have not been diminished at all because a retained life estate is one of the "strings" that causes a transferred asset to be brought back into the estate.

SPLIT INTERESTS.

Many readers will not be familiar with this phrase, but it is simple in concept: a split interest results when you keep a partial interest in an asset and give away the rest. For example, a split interest gift occurs when you give away your home but retain the right to live in it for a period of years. Here are some more sophisticated situations where charitably-inclined people give away part and keep part.

EXAMPLE 21.

Charitable gift annuity - Brent, age 80, has no spouse, children or close relatives to whom he feels inclined to leave his estate, and he has already decided to leave something to his alma mater. His income is adequate, but interest rates are low and he wouldn't mind some additional income. He contacts his alma mater's foundation and after discussing the numbers with them, decides to make a charitable gift annuity of $100,000 to the foundation. Based on his age and the interest rate in effect, Brent receives $8,000 a year for life, payable quarterly. Almost 70% of the $8,000 will be tax free; 30%, or $2,472, will be ordinary income. Plus, he gets a charitable deduction of $48,000 that he can use on his itemized income tax return over the next five years. The $100,000 will not be included in Brent's estate.

EXAMPLE 22.

Commercial annuity - Brent tells his friend, Conrad, about his charitable gift and the $8,000 a year he will be receiving. Conrad also would like more income, and Brent's charitable deduction sounds like a good deal. Conrad, who is the same age as Brent, also looks into a regular commercial annuity with a major insurance company and learns that if he invested $100,000, he will get $1,100 a month for the rest of his life.

Conrad does not have a taxable estate, his taxable income is lower than Brent's, and he is not as charitably inclined. He wants to leave as much as possible to his daughter. In addition, he hates the thought that the entire investment will be lost if he dies the next month. So he opts for an annuity for the rest of his life but with ten years certain and names his daughter as contingent beneficiary. The monthly amount is $814, which is more than Brent gets. He is willing to forego the tax benefits. This example is included to distinguish a charitable gift annuity in the previous example from the ordinary, annuitized commercial annuity having no charitable tax benefits.

EXAMPLE 23.

Charitable remainder annuity trust. (CRAT) - Daniel has a much higher net worth and income than Brent. He is also age 80 and plans to leave much larger amounts to his charities. His Certified Public Accountant has agreed to serve as trustee. Daniel opts for a charitable remainder annuity trust. He wants a steady income stream that will not fluctuate. He has highly appreciated real estate that he will use to fund the trust. The property will be sold and the net proceeds will be invested in income stocks and bonds. The terms of the trust require that 5% be distributed to him each year.

Daniel will get an income tax deduction for his charitable contribution, equal to the fair market value of the property less the value of his retained income interest. The deduction will be reduced somewhat because he donated an appreciated asset, and his charitable deduction will be limited to 30% of his adjusted gross income, spread out over the current year and as many of the following five years as are needed to utilize it.

Here are the salient features of a CRAT:

- Pays a fixed amount each year - 5% minimum by law. Distribution is mandatory, regardless of investment outcome. If the trust earns less than is distributed, its value will diminish and the charitable remainder will be less.

- Additional assets cannot be added later. Daniel would not want to donate an asset that produces no cash flow or a negative cash flow because the specified distribution has to be made each year, regardless of the trust's cash position.

EXAMPLE 24.
Charitable remainder unitrust. (CRUT) - A CRUT is similar to a CRAT in that highly-appreciated assets are usually transferred to it to avoid the capital gains tax that would result if the donor-taxpayer sold the assets and donated cash. The donor gets an income tax deduction under the IRS annuity tables and applicable federal interest rate, based on his or her age.

The payout amount for a CRUT is a fixed per cent established as established in the trust agreement (5% minimum), but it is based on the value of the trust assets at the previous year end. So the payout will fluctuate from year to year. If the value of the investments goes up, the payout goes up, and vice versa. A younger person, concerned about the long-term effects of inflation, would be more inclined to opt for a CRUT; an older person more interested in certainty and less concerned about inflation would probably be more interested in a CRAT.

One advantage of a CRUT over a CRAT is that additional contributions can be made later to a CRUT.

For purposes of valuing the gift, the older the donor, the shorter will be the donor's remaining life expectancy, the less the value of the retained interest, and the greater the value of the residual gift to the charity.

There are many other types of charitable trusts that can be used for less common situations. Again, competent tax counsel is important to avoid later disappointments.

PART V

Health Care and
Health Care Finance

CHAPTER TWELVE

HEALTH CARE DECISIONS

It is well-established law that a mentally competent adult has the right to refuse medical treatment. The problem in exercising this right arises when the person cannot communicate the decision and has not previously communicated his or her wishes to others. The law in most states presumes that you would want the full treatment. Unless your contrary wishes have previously been made known, the presumption will likely govern.

The two most common methods of communicating your wishes as to end-of-life medical decisions – the living will and the health care power of attorney – are discussed in this chapter. Note that they are both in written form. Although the medical profession will listen to the family, what if the family does not know what you would want? What if there is a disagreement between different family members? While someone's oral statements would be evidence of his or her wishes, they might not carry much weight if there was a disagreement within the family. Doctors and hospitals will be reluctant to "pull the plug," so to speak, if family unity is lacking. Decisions of this nature and magnitude are not made hastily under the best of circumstances. But if there is disagreement and nothing in writing, there will be uncertainty. An extended delay could result if the medical decision makers insist on a court order.

Another reason for expressing your wishes in writing is to be able to name the person you would want to speak on your behalf. Many states have adopted legislation that specifies the priority in which family members are to serve, in the absence of a contrary written nomination. An agent of your choosing can be appointed using a health care power of attorney. Put it in writing! And do it now, because the instrument must be signed while you are competent.

There are two types of advance directives: living wills and health care powers of attorney. These are documents outlining a patient's wishes and are to be carried out only in the event of the patient's incapacity.

LIVING WILLS.

Also called directives to physician, living wills are not wills at all in the ordinary sense of the word. They are written instructions to your physician, made while you are competent, stating how you would want end-of-life medical decisions made in the event you could not decide for yourself. What if you were permanently unconscious and unlikely to ever regain consciousness? What if you had a progressive and terminal illness - would you want life support or tube feeding in the end stages? These are just two of the many questions of this nature that couldarise. Hopefully, these scenarios will never materialize, but a living will allows you to decide in advance what you would want to occur.

One shortcoming of living wills is that state statutes are somewhat restrictive in the medical situations to which they apply. They tend to limit living wills to cases of permanent unconsciousness and of terminal illness. However, many states leave some maneuvering room by allowing the living will be in "substantially" the form specified in the statute or by providing a section for "other instructions." The unanswered question is how far one could go in adding special instructions that take the instrument well beyond the apparent legislative intent? Someone wanting to expand the scope of a living will should definitely have competent legal counsel.

Make sure that your doctor has no ethical concerns about your living will.

Another shortcoming is the difficulty of identifying and describing the medical scenarios and procedures that might be encountered in the future. It takes a certain degree of medical knowledge that neither the patient nor the attorney are likely to possess. The medical questions that will arise from Parkinson's disease will differ from those arising from Alzheimer's disease. Both will differ from those likely to arise from a congestive heart problem, etc. Someone in the health care field, such as a doctor or a home health nurse, will usually be a better resource than an attorney.

Here are some resources that will help the patient and family wrestle with questions, such as Do Not Resuscitate orders, tube feeding, ventilation, hydration, gastric tube, whether or not to administer antibiotics for pneumonia in the late stages of Alzheimer, and the like.

- **Americans for Better Care of the Dying** - This organization has published the *Handbook for Mortals: Guidance for People Facing Serious Illness*, which is an excellent reference source, written by a physician, for end-of-life care and medical questions. It covers a wide range of topics to help patients and their families from the time of diagnosis through death, including controlling of pain. Parts of the book give excellent advice that will help patients and families work better with the physician and also to draft a better living will. Excerpts from the book can be viewed at their website: www.abcd-caring.org.

- **Last Acts Partnership** - <www.partnershipforcaring.org> This organization operates a national crisis hotline (1-800-989-6455) and makes consumer pamphlets available to assist the family in discussing end-of-life decisions. The website has links to state-specific forms of living wills and health care powers of attorney.

- **Religious Organizations** - Many people make health care decisions based on their religious beliefs or affiliations. A number of religious organizations have tailored living wills to address specific concerns.

After signing a living will, give a copy to your primary care doctor and discuss it with him or her. Communication is good not only to make sure the doctor knows your sentiment, but you also want to be sure that the doctor does not have personal or professional ethical views that might interfere. You should distribute copies to other treating physicians, any hospital you have recently been treated at, and any other medical providers. Lastly, it should also be discussed with friends and relatives who are likely to be drawn into the decision making process if you are not able to communicate. Give them a copy as well. The more openly you discuss your wishes, the more likely they will be honored.

HEALTH CARE POWERS OF ATTORNEY.

It is impossible to include every possible medical scenario in a living will. Even what is anticipated may need later interpretation. "Heroic efforts" in one state will probably mean something different than "extraordinary measures" in another. It is better to go one step beyond a living will and create a health care power of attorney. A health care power of attorney allows you to appoint a health care agent to help deal with the inherent medical uncertainties. The living will serves as written expression of your values and wishes; your health care agent serves as a surrogate to interpret it and speak on your behalf.

A health care power of attorney can include provisions allowing your agent to perform such acts as: 1) give or withhold consent for surgery, medications, or other treatments, 2) make arrangements for you at hospitals, hospice, or nursing homes, and 3) authorize removal or withholding of medical treatment including artificial or technological respiration, nutrition or hydration. Another important aspect of a health care power of attorney is the provision permitting your agent to communicate with health care providers. Under recent laws, privacy rules prohibit health care providers such as doctors, hospitals, and pharmacies from releasing protected health information regarding any patient unless the information is going directly to the patient or to a representative of the patient. The representative must be appointed by the patient with a signed document, such as a health care power of attorney. This means that if the patient is incapacitated and no representative has been appointed, health care providers will be prohibited from releasing health related information to anyone, including the patient's family. By providing a valid health care power of attorney to the physician, your agent will have access to medical records, charts and other health care information.

However, someone without an intimate friend or relative to whom they could entrust end-of-life medical decisions may have no choice but to rely solely on a living will. In that case you may want to draft it with more care than someone who also has an agent.

One last point – don't forget that you can use either a living will or advance directive for health care to make it clear that you *would* want extraordinary measures taken to prolong your life! And some people do just that.

STATE REQUIREMENTS.

The forms and requirements of these planning instruments differ in almost every state. Many states have combined both the living will and health care power of attorney into one document. In some states a durable power of attorney for finances can also be used to appoint a health care agent; in other states separate forms are required. Since the legislation sanctioning these planning devices tends to be specific and often mandates a particular format, it is important that the proper form be used. And remember that the state requirements for witnessing and acceptance by the agent must be followed! Failure to comply might not fully nullify the instrument, but it will probably cause it to lose standing.

What if you move to another state? Some states will not honor a living will or health care power of attorney drafted in compliance with laws in another state. Most likely, the instruments signed in your former state will be presumed in your new state to be valid and at least given deference. Since these forms are free and readily available, the better practice would be to execute a new instrument in the form used in your new state. If you spend winters in one state and summers in another, you might want to have instruments for each state.

As stated above, you must sign a living will or health care power of attorney when you are competent. What happens if you had neither and became incapacitated? The only person who can help you at this point is a judge. This court process is called a guardianship – someone would have to petition to be appointed your guardian.

GUARDIANSHIPS.

As used in this book, the term "guardian," or "guardian of the person," refers to a court-appointed surrogate who makes medical, health care and residential living decisions for an incapacitated person. The incapacitated person traditionally has been known as the "ward" of the court. If the ward is a minor, the guardian will also make decisions with respect to the child's education and religious upbringing. A guardian serves a different role than a conservator or "guardian of the estate," who handles the ward's income and assets. (Conservators are discussed in Appendix E.)

In most states, any "interested person" can petition the court to be appointed guardian. "Interested persons" can be family members but they do not have to be. "Interested persons" can also be friends, neighbors, or even government agencies, such as adult protective services. The interested person files a petition with the court alleging that the person is not competent and asking to be appointed. The person of questionable competence is served with the petition and a notice or special summons giving him or her the opportunity to object. Next of kin and various third parties are also given notice. The petition is usually accompanied by a letter or certificate from the doctor describing the medical condition and indicating that the person is not competent. Most states also require that a third party, such as a guardian ad litem or court visitor, be appointed to inquire into the matter and report to the court. The purpose of this extra step is to reassure the court that a guardianship and the proposed guardian are appropriate. Assuming that it appears necessary and that no one objects, an uncontested order will be signed after the requisite notice period has passed. If it is an emergency situation, a temporary appointment can be obtained with a shorter notice period or even no notice. But grounds for the emergency will have to be presented.

If there is an objection, a competency hearing will be scheduled in which the testimony of the various people will be taken. The doctor's letter is obviously not binding on the court (and probably not even admissible in evidence). The standard for determining competency will vary depending on the wording of the state statute and the case law construing the statute. The issue is essentially whether the person has some type of disease, such as mental illness, retardation, Alzheimer's disease, alcoholism, etc. If so, attention is then directed to whether it incapacitates the person; i.e., renders him or her incapable of making personal decisions in his or her best interest.

Appointment of a guardian results in a great loss of personal autonomy and can be very debilitating. Recognizing this and to promote independence, modern guardianship statutes often require that the order be no more restrictive than necessary. A person might not be able to drive, for instance, but yet be fully capable of making medical or other decisions. A person might know the nature and extent of his estate and the natural objects of his bounty and thus be competent to do a will, but not be capable of making investment decisions. Note that in many states the capacity standard to enter into a contract or do business is higher than the standard to do a will.

The court order appointing a guardian (or conservator) should be tailored to the situation. BUT – if there is no objection to the petition and a guardian is appointed by default, the court order will usually grant the guardian the maximum powers allowable under the statute. This will include residential living decisions and health care and medical decisions, although the statute may deny the guardian authority to make decisions with respect to sterilization, abortion, shock therapy, and other procedures considered extreme. After the order has been signed, the court will issue "letters of guardianship," and the guardian will then be fully qualified. A bond is not normally required unless the appointment also includes authority over income and assets; i.e., a conservatorship.

It is wise to nominate someone to serve as your guardian and conservator in the event it becomes necessary. Guardianship statutes often list an order of preference for family members to serve, and the statutory preference could be at variance with yours. Even if the statute in your state is silent, you are better off to nominate someone of your own choosing. The nomination would typically be done in a financial power of attorney or health care power of attorney.

The author has made no effort throughout this book to conceal a bias against guardianships and conservatorships! They are cumbersome, and they are expensive. Use every tool in the bag to minimize the possible need – living will, health care power of attorney, durable power of attorney, living will, and anything else your attorney suggests.

CHAPTER THIRTEEN

Long-Term Care Insurance

There are a number of very valid reasons to consider long-term care insurance: to prevent impoverishment of the well spouse, to save one's estate so it can be left to desired beneficiaries, to avoid public assistance, to get a wider choice of nursing homes or assisted living facilities, and for help in paying for care at home. The long-term care insurance market is growing rapidly and will undoubtedly continue to grow as the baby boom generation starts retiring. More and more insurance companies are offering long term care policies but the decisions to be made by a consumer are difficult.

Someone with a large estate or income well beyond potential cost of long-term care doesn't need to rely on long-term care insurance – they can either self-insure or take out a policy. For those people there are some lump-sum policies with interesting features that have investment aspects and build up equity. Most seniors, of course, on are fixed and limited incomes, or will be when they retire. The comments in this chapter are directed primarily toward those who are either retired or near retirement age and who will be premium-conscious when shopping for a long-term care policy.

Younger people are also excluded from the discussion. Although coverage is available for them, the overwhelming majority of long-term care policies are sold to people in their 50s and 60s. Presumably, working-age people have little discretionary income remaining after giving priority to health insurance, life insurance, retirement savings, and disability insurance. Even if a young person has the money, it might not be wise to start paying in decades ahead of possible need – the structure of the long-term care system will undoubtedly change in the interim, quite possibly in ways that would make parts of the coverage obsolete. (The advantage of insuring early, of course, is that you are not taking the chance that a decline in health will leave you uninsurable or insurable only at high rates).

Purchasing long-term care insurance is a difficult financial decision because there are so many coverage options, and they all affect the premium. It would be nice to be able to afford a lifetime policy with full coverage and compounded inflation protection. But very few people can afford that. Most people will have to settle for less, which means deciding what objectives are most important and selecting carefully among policy features that all affect the premium.

To get the most for your money, you should have some sense of what risk or concern you are attempting to insure against. If you cannot afford full coverage, what concerns you most? This chapter is intended to give you some perspective in deciding among the various policy options.

WHAT IS LTC INSURANCE?

Although some policies pay a scheduled amount for particular services, most are indemnity type policies, meaning that they reimburse costs of care up to a certain maximum amount per day. You pay an agreed premium per month and get coverage that is limited in duration and amount. Here are the principal variables:

- **Daily benefit** - $100 per day? $300 per day? $500? Somewhere in between? The average policy benefit sold in the year 2000 was around $100 per day. Are you insuring against possible need for skilled nursing care or are you more interested in care at home? The daily benefit decision should be based on the type of care you would want most and its cost in your region.

- **Waiting period** - How long would you have to wait after going to a care facility until benefits become payable? Most policies are sold with a 90-day waiting period, but it might be better to pick a 30-day waiting period and a shorter total coverage period. This may seem counterintuitive, but, as will be seen, it is related to the effect of inflation on the cost of care and the cost of paying privately during a longer waiting period.

- **Benefit period** - How long the policy will pay? The average policy is 5.5 years but a sizeable number are sold with lifetime coverage. A longer benefit period gives peace of mind, but only a small percentage of people will need coverage for more than 5 years.

- **Inflation protection** - This option is related to the daily benefit. If the cost of care inflates at only 5% a year, it will double in 15 years. A 5% inflation rider would protect you against an erosion of benefits up to 5% per year, but your coverage would gradually become inadequate if the cost of care inflates at more than 5% a year, as some predict. Inflation protection is important, but it is also expensive.

- **Benefit trigger** - What is the standard for determining whether the insurance company has to start paying? Coverage under most policies is based on Activities of Daily Living, or "ADLs." The basic ADLs are bathing, dressing, eating, transferring from bed to chair, continence, using a toilet, and walking. The policy will define the ADLs and how many you have to fail in order to qualify for financial benefits.

  A related question is whether you need physical assistance or only supervision to accomplish the activity? Let's say that an insured is physically able to get into the bath tub but cannot be trusted to turn off the hot water due to dementia. That patient only needs supervision. If the policy required disability to the point where physical assistance is needed, the benefit trigger would not be met – at least for that ADL at that time.

- **Who determines eligibility?** - Is your eligibility determined by a letter from a physician or by a home health nurse? If the latter, is the nurse an independent contractor or an employee of the insurance company? Many insurance companies rely on Registered Nurses who are independent contractors to evaluate people for long-term care insurance coverage. The system of independent contractor nurses seems to work for life insurance physicals and should be equally acceptable for LTC insurance. It might seem comforting to think that a particular policy would allow your doctor of long standing to write a letter because he or she will probably be patient-friendly. However, the long-term care insurance industry is in its infancy. This is a much different business than life insurance, and there is much they do not know about the underwriting risks and probabilities that will apply. You would not want a company that ends up in financial straits fifteen years down the road due to lax underwriting standards just when you need the coverage. The policy might state that premiums cannot be raised, but that only means that your individual policy cannot be selectively raised. If the company gets into financial trouble and petitions the state insurance commissioner, rates for the whole class could easily get raised.

IDENTIFYING THE RISK.

Here are some statistics that might help you define your objective in taking out long-term care insurance. The figures are based on 65-year olds residing in the community in the year 2000:

- **Fifty-six per cent (56%) will never enter a nursing home.** At least the odds are that you will never need skilled nursing care. However, 44% is a very high figure, and the financial consequences can be major.

- **The 44% who will be admitted to a nursing home will not be admitted for another 18 years; i.e., not on average until age 83.** During that time the cost of care will be steadily rising.

- **Of those who do enter a nursing home, 27% will stay three months or less and 20% will stay four to twelve months.** In other words, almost half of the 44% needing care will need it for less than 12 months. The average stay for all admitees will be 2.4 years.

- **Only 19% will stay for more than five years.** This means that there is only an 8% chance that someone buying a policy at age 65 will benefit from a coverage term in excess of 5 years.

It should be noted that these figures ignore the possibility that one might need or be able to get by with a lower level of care than a nursing home, such as an assisted living facility or foster home. Nor do they reflect the possibility that in-home care might suffice. The percentages pertain only to skilled nursing facilities. In addition, slightly different statistics would apply to someone age 70 or 75 rather than age 65. So it would not be prudent to make a long-term care insurance decision based solely on the above nursing home statistics. But the statistics do, in the writer's opinion, give some perspective.

INFLATION.

Don't believe the insurance agent if he or she tells you that you don't have to worry about inflation after age 65! If that were the case, why does an inflation rider cost so much?! Inflation protection is very important. The cost of care is projected to quadruple between the year 2000 and the year 2030, which pencils out to about 5% a year, compounded annually. At an inflation rate of 5% per year, the cost of care will double every 15 years; at 6%, it will double in 12 years. Bear in mind that in addition to the basic cost of care, there will be extra expenses of perhaps 20% for drugs and supplies, the cost of which will also inflate.

Let's assume that you buy coverage of $4,000 a month at age 65 because that looks adequate in today's dollars to cover the cost of skilled nursing care in your area. The insurance agent thinks a longer coverage period would be better for you than a 5% inflation rider, since inflation protection is relatively expensive. You turn out to be average and don't need coverage until age 83. You purchased $4,000 a month 18 years prior with no inflation protection. Here is how it pencils out, assuming 5% inflation. Cost of care will have increased from $4,000 to $9,626 in 18 years at 5% (factor of 2.4). Here is your situation at the time you need care, in round figures:

Basic care	$ 9,600
+ 20% for extras	1,900
Total	$11,500
- LTC ins.	- 4,000
Out-of-pocket per mo.	$ 7,500

Without inflation protection and only $4,000 per month of coverage, you would be out-of-pocket $7,500 every month! These are rather frightening scenarios. Particularly if you are married, because your spouse will also need income to live on. With 5% inflation protection, you would at least have the basic cost of $9,600 covered.

WAITING PERIOD.

Taking the above example one step further, if you had purchased a 90-day waiting period, you would be out-of pocket almost $35,000 before the policy even started paying! ($11,500 X 3 = $34,500). You would have paid premiums for 18 years plus another $34,500 before you got any benefit from the policy. That's why, in this author's opinion, those on limited budgets should consider shortening the waiting period and adding inflation protection. The additional premium could be partially offset by shortening the total benefit period. But even by shortening the total benefit period, it might not fit into your budget.

DEFINING YOUR INSURANCE NEED.

Studies show that even a deluxe policy with 5% inflation protection is not likely to protect the estate of a middle-income person who has a long stay in a nursing home. Unless you have exceptional income or liquid assets, chances are high that you will have exhausted your liquid assets in two or three years and probably sold your home in less than five years. Those with modest income and limited liquid assets will reach those thresholds even sooner. It seems unlikely that this scenario will improve because the cost of care has been rising faster than the overall cost of living. Social Security recipients get a small cost-of-living increase, and most pensions are fixed. Nobody knows what the future rate of inflation will be for cost of care, but it is difficult to find estimates that project less than 5% per year. With the bulge of "baby boomers" in the demographic pipeline and a relatively smaller size of the work force, it seems fair to assume that cost of care will continue to inflate faster than the overall cost of living.

To get the most for your insurance dollars, you should identify your main concern or concerns and choose your policy options accordingly. Why do you want the protection? Here are some questions to consider.

- **Is your goal to preserve your estate so something will be left for your children?** This is a very worthy objective, but it might not be very realistic. Studies show that unless you have deluxe LTC coverage, a long stay in a nursing home would impoverish all but the wealthiest people. The LTC policy would pay part of the cost, income would cover part, and the balance would, of necessity, have to come from personal funds. After your cash and investments were consumed, you would be looking at selling your home or applying for Medicaid assistance.

- **Is your goal simply to be able to keep your home for a limited time in the hope that you will recover and get to come home?** Everyone who ever entered a nursing home wants to go home as soon as possible and maintains that hope longer than is realistic. As the statistics cited early in this chapter reflect, almost half of the people who enter a skilled nursing facility will stay for less than a year. It is also a statistical fact that the longer someone stays in a nursing home, the less likely it becomes that he or she will ever be able to return home. The odds start to fall off rapidly after a year in skilled nursing. So it might be more realistic to think of long-term care insurance as a means to hang onto your home while you still have a realistic prospect of being able to return to it. People on a budget might consider a shorter waiting period and shorter total benefit period of one or two years as a way to help pay for inflation protection.

Inability to carry out certain activities
of daily living qualifies a person for long-term care benefits.

- **Is your goal to remain at home as long as possible before having to go to some type of assisted living?** Some people, particularly those with a good local support system, decide that they want to stay at home regardless. These people will want to look carefully at the amount and type of in-home assistance the policy will provide. Be aware that most policies pay less for in-home care than skilled nursing care, in some cases 50% less.

- **Is your goal to protect the wealthier spouse?** As will be seen in the next chapter, if someone does not have the income and assets to pay for long-term care, public assistance in the form of Medicaid may be the only option. The problem with Medicaid is that the assets of both spouses are lumped together in determining whether the Resource Test has been met – it does not matter who owns what. The spouse with greater resources might be caught in a situation where he or she had to pay cost of care for the impoverished spouse needing care. A couple considering a second marriage late in life may want to consider long-term care insurance if one spouse has a substantial estate and the other very little. LTC insurance for the spouse with less income could avoid forcing the wealthier spouse to spend down assets to pay for the cost of care of the other spouse. They might also consider a prenuptial agreement making it clear that the assets of the spouse needing care will get spent down first, so that the well spouse can save as much as possible of his or her assets.

Again, if you have a substantial estate and don't want to self insure, it's a lot easier to decide on coverage.

CHAPTER FOURTEEN

Medicaid Assistance for the Elderly

Caveat!! This is an area where it makes no sense whatsoever to attempt to represent yourself to save legal expenses. Don't do it! If you have a parent or friend who is a candidate for public assistance for long-term care, either now or in the future, it is imperative that you find an attorney who practices regularly in this area and work with him or her. This chapter is intended merely to introduce the reader to the concepts and help in understanding the options. It is not intended to displace competent counsel.

This chapter provides an overview – and no more – of the Medicaid assistance program and the standards of eligibility for those who need long-term care but who have neither long-term care insurance nor the income or assets to pay for it. Medicaid is the source of last resort and is the only option available for many people.

Medicaid is a joint federal-state program which pays a prescribed amount for the cost of long-term care in skilled or intermediate nursing facility. In many states it also covers other types of facilities, such as adult foster homes, residential care facilities, assisted living facilities, adult day care and in-home services. Medicaid pays the care providers directly; it does not pay any cash to qualified recipients. Medicaid is a "needs-based" program; i.e., eligibility is based on factors such as financial need, age, disability status and family status.

Medicaid is often confused with Medicare, which, with its Part A and Part B, covers cost of hospitalization and medical care rather than long-term care in skilled nursing or assisted living. There is some very limited skilled nursing coverage under Medicare, but the two programs are very different. For example, if congenital heart defects run in your family and you need open-heart surgery, Medicare will cover a good portion of the cost, with no questions being asked about your income and assets. But if Alzheimer's disease is your problem and you need long-term care, don't look to Medicare for financial assistance. Your only option for public assistance will be Medicaid, and your income and assets will be critical to qualifying.

Federal law provides the basic structure of the Medicaid program. It sets certain maximums and minimums, and it mandates that certain features be included in a state plan. Federal law, however, also allows states considerable latitude in some respects. Each state establishes its own eligibility standards, and administers its own program. Therefore, the reader should be ever mindful of the fact that this area of the law is highly state-specific. Not only do the regulations vary from one state to the next, but different offices in the same state will have been known to interpret the same fact situation differently!

For ease of explanation, most of the examples assume that the husband is the Medicaid applicant (or Institutionalized Spouse) and that the wife is the Community Spouse. This will not always be the case, but the concepts are easier to explain this way.

APPLYING FOR MEDICAID.

Applications for Medicaid coverage are made with the appropriate state agency and each state will have different procedures. The applicant (or applicant's representative) will be required to show proof of residency and U.S. citizenship. Much of the application process revolves around producing financial documents such as bank statements so that the eligibility worker can determine financial eligibility. The state Medicaid agency will also perform an evaluation to determine whether the level of care required meets the minimum for eligibility.

ELIGIBILITY.

In order to qualify for Medicaid a person must pass three basic tests. First, the person must fit into a category of eligibility, meaning that he or she must be age 65 or older, be blind, or be physically or mentally disabled. A 50-year old person needing skilled or intermediate nursing care would qualify if he or she were either blind or disabled. Someone over age 65 does not have to be blind or disabled, but must need long-term care at the level being sought. After meeting the categorical eligibility test, the person must also pass both the Income Test and the Resource Test, which are the focus of this chapter.

GIFTS.

Before getting into details on the Income Test and Resource Test, the reader should understand the effect of gifts on eligibility. Gifts can greatly affect eligibility, depending on the amount, when they were made and to whom. That's because Medicaid is a needs-based program. You cannot give away your estate to your family and friends and expect to immediately qualify for Medicaid. What you gave away would have purchased a certain amount of long-term care, as a result of which you will be ineligible for a certain period of time. Gifts are not "illegal" and do not disqualify the donor forever. But they do create what is variously called a "waiting period," or "period of ineligibility" or "penalty period." After the waiting period has lapsed, the gift will no longer be an impediment to eligibility. "Gift and wait" is a strategy that is sometimes used to keep more assets in the family and also to avoid estate recovery, both of which are discussed later in the chapter.

First, let's look at some terminology that applies in the Medicaid context when a gift has been made. These terms are fundamental to understanding the effect of gifts and, as will be seen later, to devising a spend-down strategy to benefit the applicant, spouse or family.

Gift rate. Every state has what I refer to as a "gift rate," which is the average cost for one month of private-pay care in an intermediate nursing facility. The state Medicaid agencies have differing ways of establishing the private-pay rate and revise it at differing intervals. As a result, gift rates vary considerably from one state to the next. The gift rate is the basis for determining the length of the "waiting period" in the event a gift was made.

Waiting period. The length of the waiting period is equal, in months, to the value of the gift divided by the gift rate of the state in question. The waiting period begins the first day of the month that the gift was made. The examples in this chapter assume a gift rate of $4,000 per month, which might be low for a large metropolitan area and might be high for a rural area.

EXAMPLE 25.

Waiting Period - James knew that his health was failing and that long-term care was imminent. It was a high priority to him that he leave something to his children, so he made gifts to them totaling $40,000. The gift rate in James' state is $4,000. The gift caused a 10-month waiting period;

$$\$40,000 \div \$4,000 = 10$$

James will not be eligible for Medicaid assistance for ten months following the gifts. The state is assuming that the $40,000 given away would have purchased 10 months of care. It does not matter whether the gift was all to one child or was divided among several children. The gifts were not "illegal"– they only incurred a waiting period.

And it is not just gifts by the applicant. Gifts by an applicant's spouse have to be disclosed as well. If either spouse made a gift to anyone, including a child, church or charity, during the look-back period (36 months in 2004), it has to be disclosed on the application and will cause a waiting period for both spouses.

EXAMPLE 26.

Gifts by either spouse - It was the second marriage for both Susan and Clyde. They entered into a pre-nuptial agreement before their marriage, disavowing any interest in each other's estate in the event of divorce or death. They kept their finances separate because both had children by prior marriage. Susan's daughter needed $60,000 to pay off her debts, and Susan obliged. Three months later, Clyde suffered a stroke and was transferred to a nursing home a week after spending a week in the hospital. He did not have long-term care insurance, and his resources ran out in three months. With a gift rate of $4,000, the waiting period for a $60,000 gift is 15 months. Six months have passed since the gift, so it will be another 9 months before he will qualify for Medicaid assistance. The state is not bound by the prenuptial agreement. A waiting period is imposed on Clyde, even though it was Susan who made the gift.

In some states, the daughter could give back the portion of the gift representing the remainder of the waiting period, $36,000 in this case. Susan could use it for Clyde's cost of care and then qualify him; provided, of course, that the Income Test and Resource Tests discussed below were otherwise satisfied. In other states, the daughter would have to give the full $60,000 back. But if the daughter no longer had the money or was not inclined to part with it, Clyde would not be eligible for Medicaid assistance for another 9 months. His only option would be to apply for a hardship waiver, which the state Medicaid agency would probably review with a certain degree of bias.

Look-back period. Reference was made above to the look-back period. When someone applies for Medicaid assistance, the state Medicaid agency has the right to look at financial records over the previous 36 months. This is known as the "look-back" period. All gifts (and bargain sales) made during the 36-month look-back period must be disclosed on the application – intentional failure to disclose it would be fraud if it resulted in qualifying an applicant who would not otherwise have qualified. This does not mean that the applicant will be disqualified for the full 36 months, because that depends on the value of the gift divided by the gift rate in effect at the time. The look-back period is 60 months in the case of gifts to or from a trust.

It's easy to confuse the look-back period with the waiting period. This example will help differentiate between them:

EXAMPLE 27.

Waiting period vs. look-back period - It was a high priority to Frank that he pass on the bulk of his estate to his daughter, Rachel. He had Parkinson's disease and his health was failing. He was concerned that the cost of long-term care would consume all of his assets. So he gifted his home worth $320,000 to Rachel to avoid probate – it would go to her under his will anyway. A year after the gift, his Parkinson's disease had progressed to the point where he had to be placed in an expensive residential care facility. Twenty five months later, his countable assets (discussed below) for Medicaid purposes were down to $2,000. It has now been 37 months since the gift. With a gift rate of $4,000, the waiting period would technically run for 80 months ($320,000 ÷ $4,000). However, since more than 36 months has lapsed since the gift, the look-back period has expired. The gift does not even have to be disclosed on the application. Frank would be eligible in the 37th month, regardless of the amount of the gift. The look-back period is capped at 36 months under present law, so gifts more than 36 months prior to the application are disregarded.

But note that the waiting period can be indefinite in length. If a large gift is made and a Medicaid application is made before the look-back period has expired, the waiting period is potentially unlimited. In this example, if someone made the mistake of filing an application for Frank 35 months after the gift, the caseworker would presumably say, "A gift was made during the look-back period, and the waiting period is 80 months. Come back in 45 months."

The look-back period for gifts to or from trusts is 60

months. If Frank had owned his home in a revocable living trust and deeded it directly from the trust to Susan, he would not be eligible for 60 months. Under those circumstances, he would want to first deed the home from the trust back to himself and then to his daughter, which would lower the look-back period to 36 months.

The last example also highlights one very basic fact of Medicaid law: while the home is an exempt asset, giving it away will result in a waiting period. In addition, although the home is exempt, proceeds from its sale are not exempt because cash is a countable asset.

Exceptions – gifts to favored family members. Not all gratuitous transfers are treated as gifts. Certain gifts are exempt by definition and do not result in a waiting period. These exceptions are sometimes an appropriate way to transfer countable assets to another family member and get the applicant qualified sooner. And, as discussed later in this chapter, they can also be useful in avoiding estate recovery:

The home can be transferred to the applicant's:

- **Spouse**

- **Minor child** (under the age of 21)

- **Blind child** (any age)

- **Permanently and totally disabled child** (any age) – i.e., eligible for Social Security Disability (SSD)

- **Adult child who is residing in the parent's home and who provided care for at least two consecutive years before the Medicaid applicant was institutionalized.** Federal law recognizes the value of keeping people at home as long as possible, and the fact is that many children step up to the plate to take care of their aging parents. To encourage this, an exception to the law on gifting exists where a child takes care of his or her parent. If the child lives under the same roof and takes care of the parent for two continuous years and if the care provided kept the parent out of the institution, transfer of the home to the child will not be treated as a gift.

This exception might be restrictively construed to require that the child live under the same roof – living in a guest house, in a second mobile home or above the garage might not qualify, depending on the regulations of the state in question. State regulations differ and always have to be consulted. In addition, care should be taken to be able to document which activities of daily living the parent would fail.

Hopefully, if the parent is not competent to transact business, a durable power of attorney will exist which authorizes the agent to make the gift to the care-giver child. If not, a court order might be needed.

- **Sibling** who has an equity interest in the home and resided in the home for at least one year immediately before the Medicaid applicant was institutionalized. There is no requirement that the sibling have provided care.

Unlimited assets of any kind, including cash, can be transferred to certain family members who are favored under Medicaid law without incurring a waiting period:

- **Spouse.** This is not the gaping loophole that it might seem to be because all assets of both spouses, however titled, are lumped together for purposes of applying the Resource Test, discussed below. Transfers to the spouse become the basis for many strategies for protecting assets.

- **Minor child** (under the age of 21)

- **Blind child** (any age)

- **Permanently and totally disabled child** (any age) i.e., eligible for Social Security Disability (SSD)

EXAMPLE 28.

Gift to disabled child - Charles and Molly owned their home plus a rental home worth $200,000, which is a countable asset. Their daughter, Betsy, receives Social Security Disability Income due to her disability. Betsy lives independently. Molly needs skilled nursing care but the couple's assets are well over the limit due to the rental house. They deed the rental home to Betsy. This gratuitous transfer is not regarded as a disqualifying gift under the Medicaid laws, so there is no waiting period. Cash could also be given to her. Betsy gets the rental home and rental income, and the rental home is no longer a countable asset to the parents. If Betsy chose to live in the home, it would not affect her Supplemental Security Income (SSI). However, the utilities, taxes, insurance and maintenance would somehow have to be paid, and Betsy presumably would not have the income to do so.

The above exceptions to gifting are the foundation for many spend-down strategies designed to hasten someone's eligibility for Medicaid and keep more assets within the family.

RESOURCE TEST.

Medicaid is a needs-based program, meaning that wealthy people need not bother to apply. In addition to falling within one of the categories of eligibility (over age 65, minor, blind, disabled, etc.), a Medicaid applicant must pass both a Resource Test and an Income Test. Let's examine the Resource Test first. An applicant can own an unlimited amount of exempt assets but only a maximum of $2,000 ($3,000 for a married couple when both are applicants for benefits) of non-exempt or "countable" assets. The first step in reviewing someone's eligibility situation is to categorize each asset as either exempt or countable. The Resource Test will be applied somewhat differently from one state to the next, but the following is typical.

Exempt assets include the following:

- One home, as long as the applicant lives there or intends to return to it, or as long as the spouse or a minor, blind,

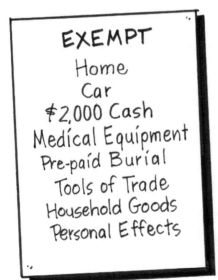

The Resource Test helps determine Medicaid eligibility.

or disabled child lives in it. In some states the home cannot be held in a trust. This is a very complex topic about which more will be said because preserving the family home is a very important goal for most people. For present purposes, suffice it to say that an applicant can have unlimited equity in a home and still qualify for Medicaid. This does not mean that the state might not be able to place a lien against it for reimbursement or to recover from the recipient's estate after death for the Medicaid assistance provided. Nor does it mean that the Medicaid recipient will necessarily be allowed to continue owning the home indefinitely, as the state might eventually want it sold if protracted care is required.

- One motor vehicle with equity up to $4,500. However, the equity can be unlimited if: 1) the vehicle is used for employment, 2) it is used for medical treatment, 3) it is a specifically-modified vehicle, or 4) circumstances require a vehicle. If there is a spouse living in the community, a vehicle of any value is exempt.

- Household items, such as furniture or furnishings.

- Personal effects, which in some states is subject to a $2,000 limit (but the limit may not be strictly enforced).

- Medical equipment for either spouse – unlimited in amount.

- Hardgoods for burial (lot, casket, liner, headstone).

- $1,500 can be set aside in an interest-accumulating savings account dedicated as a "burial fund" or any "revocable" funeral arrangement up to a $1500 limit or a life insurance policy with less than $1,500 face value. An irrevocable funeral arrangement with no surrender value works in some states to get around the low limit. Term life insurance policies are not countable assets because they have no cash surrender value.

- Property used in the applicant's or spouse's trade or business and necessary for support.

- Tools of the applicant's or spouses' trade.

- A maximum of $2,000 in cash or other countable resources (or $3,000 if both spouses are applying). This is the category that gets the most attention because investments, including the cash surrender value of life insurance, in excess of $2,000, are countable.

Countable assets include everything convertible into cash which does not fit into one of the exempt categories. Countable assets include all of the following types of assets:

- All real estate other than the home (but in some states the home is countable if held in a trust).

- Liquid assets, such as checking and savings accounts, stocks, bonds, cash surrender value of life insurance, except $2,000 ($3,000 if both spouses are applying).

- IRAs, 401(k)s, 403(b)s, etc. - A few states treat tax-deferred balances as exempt. Most states look at accessibility – that is, could the owner demand the balance? If so, the balance, less any income tax liability, will be treated as a countable resource.

    If the applicant is 70 ½, he or she is required to take mandatory annual distributions, and the account might be categorized as income rather than a countable asset. If the applicant had purchased an annuity in an IRA and made an irrevocable election for monthly payments for life, for instance, the distributions would be treated as income.

- Joint bank accounts with people other than the spouse are presumed to belong to the Medicaid applicant, unless the child or other joint owner can prove how much he or she contributed to the account. If the applicant and other joint owner each contributed half, then only half would be a countable asset. Note that if the applicant contributed 100% and the other joint owner has withdrawn any funds during the look-back period, the withdrawal will be considered to be a gift from the applicant as of the time of the withdrawal.

- Land sale contracts, trust deeds and promissory notes. The balance is countable if there is a demand feature. However, if regular payments are being received, the asset might be categorized as income.

Unavailable assets are assets that for one reason or another could not be converted to cash. They not exempt assets but might not be counted for eligibility purposes. A person might be given conditional eligibility and be required produce documentation from time to time to maintain eligibility.

- Real property which is jointly owned with someone other than the spouse will usually be treated as "not available," at least if the other joint owner provides a letter or affidavit to the effect that he or she is unwilling to sell. Again, this is not to say that the state Medicaid agency might not be able to place a lien against the Medicaid recipient's interest or be able to recover after death from his or her estate.

- Unmarketable property will not be counted as available. However, you have to look closely at state regulations to determine what form of proof will be required to establish lack of marketability.

The examples throughout this chapter assume that none of the assets are "unavailable;" i.e., all assets are either exempt or countable.

Countable assets - single persons. For an unmarried Medicaid applicant, determining total countable assets is a relatively straightforward matter of identifying assets and placing them in either the "exempt" column or the "countable" column. Only if the value of the countable assets is less than $2,000 will an unmarried applicant qualify for Medicaid. Spending, re-positioning or, in some cases, gifting the assets in excess of $2,000 is known as the "spend-down," a topic about which much more will be said.

Countable assets - married couples. For married couples, if only one spouse is applying for benefits, the Resource Test is more complicated. The process of categorizing assets as exempt or countable is the same, except that if the Medicaid applicant is married, the assets of both spouses will be added together. It makes no difference how they are titled. Title could be in the wife's name, in the husband's name or be jointly owned – all countable assets will be pooled together. Even separate assets that the Community Spouse owned before the marriage and even if there is a pre-nuptial agreement! However, as will be seen, in "Protecting the Community Spouse," starting at page 172, the Community Spouse is entitled to a share of the countable assets, known as the Community Spouse Resource Allowance (CSRA), which he or she gets to keep. It does not have to be spent down.

EXAMPLE 29.
Exempt vs. countable assets

	Exempt	Countable
Him		
Savings		$15,000
Stocks		20,000
Her		
Real estate contract		50,000
Annuity (not in payout)		25,000
Joint		
Home (all equity)	X	
Checking	2,000	5,000
Car	X	

This couple has $115,000 in countable assets. This figure becomes the basis for calculating the Community Spouse Resource Allowance, which is discussed in "Protecting the Community Spouse," starting at page 172

INCOME TEST.

In addition to passing the Resource Test, a Medicaid applicant must pass the Income Test. Congress set the maximum income for a Medicaid applicant at three times the Supplemental Security Income (SSI) standard, the latter being a monthly income amount below which Congress feels no person should fall. The SSI standard is adjusted annually for inflation, based on the Consumer Price Index. The SSI figure for the year 2005 is $579 per month, so the income cap figure for a Medicaid applicant is $1,737 in most states.

EXAMPLE 30.

Income test–income cap - Michael is single. He needs intermediate nursing care, which will cost $3,500 per month. Michael owns only his clothing, furniture, car and less than $2,000 in cash, so he passes the Resource Test. His income consists of Social Security of $1,200 per month and a pension of $300 per month. Since his income is less than the $1,737 limit, he also passes the Income Test.

If his total income were more than $1,737, he technically would not pass the Income Test. The consequence of excess income will vary, depending on whether he lives in a "medically needy" state or an "income cap" state. In a medically needy state, income in excess of $1,737 will not be an impediment to his qualification for Medicaid. In those states, Michael would get a small personal needs allowance, probably $30, and the rest of his income would go toward his cost of care, with the state Medicaid program picking up the difference.

In an "income cap" state, an income cap trust (also known as a "Miller" trust) might have to be set up to accomplish the same result.

WHAT COUNTS AS INCOME?

"Income," for Medicaid purposes, is defined somewhat differently than it is for income tax purposes or under generally accepted accounting principles. Medicaid income basically includes all amounts of money received on a regular basis. Pension payments and Social Security are obviously income. If the applicant had an annuity and had made an irrevocable election to take fixed monthly payments for the remainder of his life, Medicaid would classify the payments as income, even though the Internal Revenue Service might classify most of the payments as return of capital rather than income. If, however, he gave instructions to distribute the annuity interest monthly and was free to cancel his instructions or demand the entire annuity balance, the entire balance would be available and classified as a countable asset.

Note that for purposes of applying the Income Test and Resource Test, an item normally will be categorized as either an asset or as income, but not both.

Determining income where there is a spouse. You will recall that the assets of both spouses are lumped together in applying the Resource Test. It doesn't matter which spouse owns what – everything gets added together. Income is handled differently. In calculating income, income is separated according to the name on the check. All income in the applicant's name is attributable to the applicant, and all income in the Community Spouse's name is attributed to the Community Spouse. Income in the names of both spouses is divided equally. This is an important point to remember because if the Community Spouse (CS) has high income, he or she is not obligated to use it to support the Medicaid applicant.

EXAMPLE 31.

Income test–income of spouse - Martin receives a monthly pension of $900 and Social Security of $600. His wife, Karen, receives a pension of $2,100 a month and Social Security of $1,300. In addition, Karen sold some real property, and the monthly contract payments of $800 come in her name only. Martin needs intermediate nursing care. His income is $1,500, so he passes the Income Test. It does not matter that Karen's income is $4,200 – Karen, the CS, is not obligated to support Martin in the nursing home.

EXAMPLE 32.

Income test–name on check - Income is attributable to the person whose name is on the check. If the $800 contract payments in Example 31 came in the names of both Martin and Karen, half would be attributed to Martin and half to Karen. Their incomes would be as follows:

	Karen	Martin
Pension	$2,100	$ 900
Soc. Sec.	1,300	600
Contract pymts. on sale of home	400	400

In this case, Martin could assign his interest in the promissory note and mortgage to Karen so the checks would come in her name only. Gratuitous transfers between spouses do not trigger a waiting period. Assigning the note and mortgage would lower Martin's income to $1,500 and raise Karen's income from $3,800 to $4,200. Martin is now below the income cap, and the additional income to Karen would not affect Martin's eligibility.

Note that Social Security cannot be assigned, and a cumbersome Qualified Domestic Relations Order would be required to split or assign the applicant's pension income. Also, Medicaid will count as income funds which the Medicaid applicant is entitled to but does not receive.

PROTECTING THE COMMUNITY SPOUSE

In 1988, Congress passed the Medicare Catastrophic Coverage Act (MCCA), the aim of which was to apply the income and resources of the spouse needing Medicaid assistance toward cost of care, but to do so without totally impoverishing the Community Spouse. MCCA established two important rights for the Community Spouse. First, the Community Spouse is entitled to certain minimum monthly income, known as the Minimum Monthly Maintenance Needs Allowance (MMMNA). If the Community Spouse's separate income is not sufficient to reach the MMMNA, then the Community Spouse may be entitled to receive some income from the Medicaid recipient's monthly income, which amount is called the Community Spouse Monthly Income Allowance (CSMIA). Second, the Community Spouse is also entitled to a share of the couple's total countable assets, known as the Community Spouse Resource Allowance (CSRA).

Community Spouse Monthly Income Allowance. As explained above, the Community Spouse gets to keep all of his or her income in almost every state. If Mrs. Jones happens to have a high monthly pension, for example, she is not expected to use it to subsidize Mr. Jones' nursing home costs. However, if Mrs. Jones has very little of her own income, she may be entitled to a portion of Mr. Jones' monthly income. This concept, known as the Community Spouse Monthly Income Allowance (hereafter "CSMIA"), is not to be confused with the income cap figure, which applies only to the Medicaid applicant. It is Mrs. Jones' right to a certain minimum monthly income. If her actual income is below the minimum, she will be entitled to some of Mr. Jones' income – but only if it exists. The CSMIA is not an entitlement in the sense that the government would pay her a subsidy. It is only the right to a portion of Mr. Jones' income – if he had no income, Mrs. Jones would get nothing.

The starting point for calculating the CSMIA is determining the MMMNA amount. The MMMNA is the basic support figure set by federal law plus an Excess Shelter Allowance. The basic support figure amount ($1,561 for 2004-2005) is the federal poverty level income for a family of two and is adjusted mid-year for inflation. The Excess Shelter Allowance is the amount by which the Community Spouse's shelter expenses exceed 30% of the basic support figure. Shelter expenses include rent or mortgage, taxes and insurance, a standard utility allowance and maintenance or homeowner's association fee.

The Excess Shelter Allowance in 2005 is calculated as follows:

+	Rent or mortgage payment
+	RP taxes if own home (or if lease requires payment)
+	Casualty insurance
+	Standard utility allowance
	(winter rate or summer rate set by state)
- 468	Shelter standard (30% of $1,561)
=	Excess Shelter Allowance

The CSMIA is calculated by deducting the actual income of the Community Spouse from the MMMNA (the sum of the basic support figure plus the Excess Shelter Allowance):

$1,561	Basic support figure
+	Excess Shelter Allowance
=	MMMNA
-	Actual income of Community Spouse
=	Community Spouse Monthly Income Allowance

EXAMPLE 33.

Community Spouse Monthly Income Allowance - James suffered a stroke and was admitted to a nursing facility after discharge from the hospital. Based on their modest income and resources, James qualifies for Medicaid assistance. His income consists of $1,600 Social Security. The income of his wife, Cecilia, is $320 Social Security. They rent an apartment for $600 per month. The standard utility allowance in their state is $300. A Medicaid recipient in their state gets a personal needs allowance of $30 per month.

Cecilia's Excess Shelter Allowance is $432:

$600	Rent or mortgage payment
0	RP taxes if own home
	(or if lease requires payment)
0	Casualty insurance
300	Standard utility allowance
	(winter rate or summer rate set by state)
-468	Shelter standard
$432	Excess Shelter Allowance

Cecilia's CSMIA is $1,673:

$1,561	Basic support figure
+ 432	Excess Shelter Allowance
- 320	Actual income of Community Spouse
= $ 1,673	CSMIA

James' income is $1,600 and the first $30 goes to James for his personal needs allowance, leaving $1,570 left for Cecilia. Even though her CSMIA is $1,673, Cecilia gets only $1,570 – the government does not make up the difference.

EXAMPLE 34.

Community Spouse Monthly Income Allowance - Same figures, except that James and Cecilia own a home free and clear. Taxes and insurance are $200 per month and casualty insurance is $40. Cecilia's Excess Shelter Allowance is only $71:

$ 0	Rent or mortgage payment
200	RP taxes if own home
	(or if lease requires payment)
40	Casualty insurance
300	Standard utility allowance
	(winter rate or summer rate set by state)
- 468	Shelter standard
$ 72	Excess Shelter Allowance

Cecilia's CSMIA is $1,313:

$1,561	Basic Support Figure
+ 72	Excess Shelter Allowance
- 320	Actual income of Community Spouse
= $ 1,313	CSMIA

The CSMIA is typically smaller for those who own their own home. The first $30 of James' income goes for his personal needs allowance, the next $1,313 goes to Cecilia, and the rest of James' income goes toward his cost of care.

The Minimum Monthly Maintenance Needs Allowance is capped at $2,377 (2004-2005 figure):

EXAMPLE 35.

Community Spouse Monthly Income Allowance - Phillip suffered a stroke and was admitted to a nursing home after discharge from the hospital. He qualifies for Medicaid assistance. Phillip's income is $2,500 per month, and his cost of care will be $4,000. The income of Patti, his wife, is $360 Social Security. They own their own home but it is mortgaged for $1,150 per month. Taxes are $250 per month and casualty insurance is $50. The standard utility allowance in their state is $300. A Medicaid recipient in their state gets a personal needs allowance of $30 per month.

Patti's Excess Shelter Allowance is $1,282:

$1,150	Rent or mortgage payment
250	RP taxes if own home
	(or if lease requires payment)
50	Casualty insurance
300	Standard utility allowance
	(winter rate or summer rate set by state)
-468	Shelter standard
$ 1,282	Excess Shelter Allowance

Patti's CSMIA would be $2,483 if it were not capped:

$1,561	Basic support figure

+ 1,282	Excess Shelter Allowance
- 360	Actual income of Community Spouse
= $ 2,483	CSMIA

Although Patti's CSMIA calculates to $2,483, it is capped by law at $2,377 for the year 2004, and the Medicaid caseworker cannot allow more. The first $30 of Phillip's income goes to his personal needs allowance, Patti gets the next $2,377, and the rest is applied to Phillip's cost of care.

Increasing the CSMIA. The Community Spouse is entitled to receive and keep her own income plus her CSMIA as calculated above, without respect to her actual living costs. Sometimes the Community Spouse is frugal or has minimal living expenses and can get by on that amount. But often that is not the case. Medicaid law has provisions to accommodate hardship situations without requiring a divorce or separation. All states allow for an administrative hearing to establish a hardship case. A substantial number of states also allow the Community Spouse to petition the state court for a support order increasing the CSMIA if, based on her actual living costs, she needs more income. A petition for support (which is neither a divorce nor separation) is most likely to be helpful when the Community Spouse has high costs of living due to high medical expenses, high debt, high mortgage payments, extraordinary household expenses. (And we continue to assume that the Institutionalized Spouse has income to transfer, because the Medicaid program will not pay cash to the CS). Although it is also possible to get the CSMIA increased through an administrative hearing before the state Medicaid agency, many attorneys who practice in this area would prefer to have the matter heard before a judge in the state court.

EXAMPLE 36.

Increasing the CSMIA - Ralph was admitted to a skilled nursing facility and application was made for Medicaid assistance. His combined income from pension and Social Security is $2,300. His wife, Monica, has income of $320. They rent an apartment for $600 per month. The standard utility allowance in their state is $300. A Medicaid recipient in their state gets a personal needs allowance of $30 per month.

Monica's Excess Shelter Allowance is $432:

$600	Rent or mortgage payment
0	RP taxes if own home
	(or if lease requires payment)
0	Casualty insurance
300	Standard utility allowance
	(winter rate or summer rate set by state)
- 468	Shelter standard = 30% of poverty level
	income ($1,561 in 2004)
$432	Excess Shelter Allowance

Monica's regularly-calculated CSMIA would be $1,673:

$1,561	Basic Support Figure
+ 432	Excess Shelter Allowance
- 320	Actual income of Community Spouse
= $ 1,673	CSMIA

The problem is that Monica needs more than $1,673 due to her extremely high pharmaceutical expenses. Their state allows petitions for support. Monica contacts an attorney experienced in this area of the law. Based on her actual, itemized costs of living, she petitions the state court to increase her CSMIA, giving notice to the state Medicaid agency. The proceeding is neither a divorce nor a legal separation. Since Ralph is not competent, a guardian ad litem (such as Ralph's child) will have to be appointed to counsel him. With the approval of the guardian ad litem, a court order is entered raising Monica's CSMIA to, let's say, $1,950. The first $30 of Ralph's income goes for his personal needs, the next $1,950 goes to Monica, and the rest goes to Ralph's cost of care.

To avoid unduly complicating the income calculations, the above examples ignore the charge for Medicare, Part B ($78.20 in 2005), which is deducted from their Social Security checks. The premium for Medicare, Part B gets added to their incomes and then deducted out. Readers interested in the way Medicaid works should also be aware that the Community Spouse is treated less favorably in many states if the ill spouse has limited income and goes to an adult foster home, assisted living facility, or other community-based facility, as opposed to skilled or intermediate nursing care. A significant charge for board and room could be deducted from the income of the Institutionalized Spouse as a higher priority than the CSMIA, which could reduce the amount available for the Community Spouse.

PREPAID BURIAL INSURANCE?
MEDICAL SUPPLIES?
PAY OFF MORTGAGE?
ANNUITY?
GIFTS?
NEW CAR?

Medicaid is one area where it makes no sense whatsoever to attempt to represent yourself to save legal expenses.

Community Spouse Resource Allowance. The other anti-impoverishment concept introduced by the Medicare Catastrophic Coverage Act of 1988 is the Community Spouse Resource Allowance. The Community Spouse is entitled to keep a certain share of the couple's countable assets. That share, known as the "Community Spouse Resource Allowance," is the largest of:

1. One half the total countable assets, subject to the maximum. Congress set a minimum and a maximum which is adjusted for inflation each year. For 2005, the minimum is $19,020, and the maximum is $95,100. These are the figures within which the fifty states must set their minimums and maximums. A state can set the minimum at more than $19,020 but not less. A state cannot set the maximum at more than $95,100 (2005 figure). A few states have chosen to set their minimums at the federal maximum of $95,100, so that the minimum and maximum are the same in those states; i.e., the first $95,100 of countable assets go to the Community Spouse. Most states have adopted the federal standard as their minimum, and the examples use the federal standard as the minimum.

EXAMPLE 37.
Community Spouse Resource Allowance - Paul and Sylvia own their home, a car and savings of $100,000. The home and car are exempt, so their countable assets are $100,000. The Community Spouse Resource Allowance is half, or $50,000, and the Medicaid applicant would get to keep $2,000 of countable assets as his Personal Needs Allowance. In most states, they would have to "spend down" $48,000 (half of $100,000 less $2,000) in some manner to qualify either spouse for Medicaid assistance. If they were lucky and lived in one of the states that sets the minimum the same as the maximum, the CSRA would be $95,100 and only $2,900 would have to be spent down ($100,000 less $95,100 less $2,000).

EXAMPLE 38.

CSRA Maximum - If the countable assets of Paul and Sylvia were $200,000, half would be $100,000. However, the Community Spouse would not get to keep the full $100,000 due to the maximum. The maximum Community Spouse Resource Allowance is $95,100 (2005 figure). The difference ($200,000 less $95,100 less $2,000 = $102,900) would have to be spent down in some manner.

CSRA Minimum - On the other hand, if total countable assets were $20,000, the minimum CSRA would enter in. Paul gets to keep $2,000 as his Personal Needs Allowance, which leaves $18,000. Since the minimum CSRA for 2005 is $19,020, Sylvia would get to keep the entire $18,000, and nothing would have to be spent down.

Snapshot. The medicaid agency looks at the countable resources to determine the CSRA on the first day of continuous care, which is sometimes the date of the Medicaid application and sometimes the earlier date of institutionalization. This is often referred to as a "snapshot," and it becomes the basis for determining the CSRA. Bank, insurance and brokerage statements from that snapshot month must be produced so the eligibility worker can make the calculations.

EXAMPLE 39.

CSRA Snapshot - Eight months ago, Paul was admitted to a nursing home and has been residing there since. Sylvia is now applying for Medicaid for Paul. The Medicaid worker determines that the CSRA snapshot is to be taken eight months ago when Paul was first institutionalized and asks for financial statements from that month. Eight months ago, Sylvia and Paul had $64,000 in available assets but now only have $32,000 due to the $4000 per month nursing home bill. The Medicaid worker sets the CSRA at $32,000 (one-half of $64,000). Because Sylvia and Paul's available assets are down to $32,000, Paul is resource eligible, and further spend down is not required.

2. The amount specified in an administrative or court order. The federal statute provides that if the Community Spouse can establish that the income from her CSRA does not generate enough income to raise her total income to the minimum ($1,561 in 2004-2005), the CSRA can be increased to give her additional income-generating resources. However, before transferring assets, most states require the income of the Institutionalized Spouse be transferred first ("income first" rule). There has been considerable litigation on this point, and for the most part states have been allowed to require income to be transferred before assets. If the income of the Community Spouse, after transferring the maximum available amount of his income, is still below the minimum to which she is entitled, then assets can be transferred to provide additional income.

EXAMPLE 40.
Increasing the CSRA for extra income - Mr. Emerson, who qualifies medically for Medicaid, receives Social Security of $500 and a pension of $400. Mrs. Emerson receives Social Security of $300. Their only countable asset is a mutual fund of corporate bonds having a value of $100,000 and yielding 4%. Their spend-down amount is $48,000 (half of $100,000 less $2,000).

Mrs. Emerson's MMMNA is the basic $1,561 (2004 figure), and her income is $300, so she is entitled to an additional $1,261 (if it exists, of course). The state follows the income-first rule, so Mr. Emerson's income must be transferred before her CSRA can be increased. All of Mr. Emerson's $900 monthly income (except his $30 personal needs allowance) will go to

Mrs. Emerson. The $870 from Mr. Emerson's income raises her income to only $1,170 per month, which is still $391 short of $1,561. The 4% bond fund generates monthly income of $333, so her CSRA can be increased to $98,000. Even with the $333 of additional income from the bond fund, her total income is less than $1,561. The net result of increasing her CSRA is that she gets both the bond fund and the income it generates.

Whether Mrs. Emerson's CSRA can be increased without an administrative hearing or court order will depend on the regulations of the state in question. In a simple case like this, where the combined income of both spouses is less than the basic support figure and transfer of all available income of the Institutionalized Spouse to the Community Spouse still leaves a shortfall, many state Medicaid agencies would allow an informal increase in the CSRA without an administrative hearing or court order. Others would not do it informally but would honor a court order that raised the CSRA.

It is obviously to the advantage of the Community Spouse to get the Resource Allowance as high as possible – this gives her both the asset plus the income and leaves her in a better posture should the Institutionalized Spouse die. Her income would not drop as sharply if the Institutionalized Spouse were to die, as it often does in the cases where pension income is involved. Transferring assets to the Community Spouse could postpone having to dip into tax-deferred assets, such as IRAs or tax-deferred annuities. It's always better to have both the income and the asset itself.

SPEND-DOWN STRATEGIES.

We are now to the point in the process where, with the assistance of either a knowledgeable attorney or a Medicaid caseworker, you know what assets existed on the day continuous care started; i.e., the snapshot date when the applicant went to the hospital or nursing home. You also know which assets are exempt, and the total of countable assets. If the applicant has a spouse, you also know the amounts of the Community Spouse Resource Allowance and Community Spouse Monthly Income Allowance and how much must be spent down. The question is how to best spend the excess of countable assets. One option, of course, is to pay for cost of care privately until countable assets have fallen far enough. Some people choose to do that as a matter of principle, and others do it out of ignorance. The discussion that follows assumes that you want to consider other options.

For unmarried applicants. Let's start with an unmarried applicant because the spend-down options for a single person are fairly limited and straight-forward. Spending down is essentially a question of deciding what to do with the countable assets in excess of $2,000. The goal is to enhance the quality of the applicant's life and, secondarily, to preserve assets and/or income for others in the family. Here are some of the ways that countable assets in excess of $2,000 can be spent:

1. **Buy prepaid burial insurance and burial hard goods** – This should be considered for every applicant, whether married or single. In the alternative a $1500 burial account can be opened for the applicant and their spouse.

2. **Pay off debt and credit cards.**

3. **Purchase medical equipment and supplies.**

4. **Purchase clothing, new television, furniture and other con-**

sumer items, such as room decorations, talking book or magazine subscriptions, Netflix.com subscription, long distance calling cards, hobby materials, etc.

5. **Liquidate tax-deferred accounts.** If any of the countable assets are in an IRA or other tax-deferred plan, liquidate it and prepay the tax liability. (Almost all states treat tax-deferred accounts as countable assets).

6. **Pay family members for assistance.** This keeps money in the family, but it has to be pursuant to a written agreement. And the payments will be taxable income to the recipient.

There are numerous spend-down strategies for Medicaid situations.

7. **Buy an annuity.** This strategy has limited application for unmarried applicants as it will work only if the payout election includes a period certain and only if the Medicaid recipient dies before the payout period ends. Even then, the state might recover part or all of the remaining payments after the death of the Medicaid recipient.

EXAMPLE 41.

Annuity converts resource into income - Clyde is single, is terminally ill and needs long-term care. His son has taken care of him for a long time but can no longer provide the level of care that Clyde needs. Clyde is very grateful for the care he has received and is concerned that cost of care will consume his remaining estate and nothing will be left for his only child. He purchases an annuity sufficient to lower his countable assets to $2,000 and makes an irrevocable election to receive payments over the next 5 years and naming his son as contingent beneficiary. The right to the payments is not assignable under the terms of the policy. Clyde's life expectancy under the Social Security mortality table is 6 years.

Clyde qualifies for Medicaid assistance because what was previously a countable resource is now regarded as income. (However, the income from the annuity will be applied toward his cost of care). After his death, his son may receive the payments for the remainder of the 5 years.

However, estate recovery might enter in here! If Clyde passed away after two years of payments, the state, depending on the regulations it had adopted, could assert a claim to part of the remaining payments based on Clyde's life expectancy the day before his death, which would be three and a fraction years. In that case, the state would recover its cash outlays first, and his son would receive the payments for the remainder of the three years, if any.

Aside from possible estate recovery considerations, annuities don't appeal to most single applicants because the implicit assumption is that the applicant will not survive the payout period. This is an unpleasant thought for the family. It's often better to use the "half-a-loaf" gifting strategy.

8. **Gifting - "half-a-loaf."** The idea is to give away a calculated amount and hold back enough to cover cost of care and extras until the waiting period expires. It's not as good as keeping everything, but it's better than nothing!

EXAMPLE 42.

Gift of "half a loaf" - Mary is single and needs intermediate nursing care. She has countable assets of $30,000, so $28,000 has to be spent down. The gift rate in her state is $3,500, her cost of care is $3,000 a month, and extras at the nursing home will be approximately $500 more. Her daughter has helped take care of her over the past year, for which Mary is very appreciative. Mary decides to give her daughter $14,000, holding back $16,000. Four months later, after paying $14,000 privately for cost of care and extras, the waiting period has passed. Her countable assets are below $2,000, and she qualifies for Medicaid. Her daughter has $14,000 that otherwise would have gone to cost of care.

Note that if Mary happened to make the gift 4 months before she even needed long-term care, her countable assets when care was needed would be down to $16,000. She could give an additional $7,000 to her daughter at that time and hold back $9,000 to pay privately. After two months of private pay, her countable assets would be down to $2,000, the waiting period would have expired, and she would qualify for Medicaid. Her daughter would have $21,000 of her original $30,000, rather than $14,000. The problem, of course, is that you never know when in the future you will need long-term care.

Gifting is not a strategy that is highly recommended because it carries with it a loss in one's feeling of security. To constitute a gift, their transfer must be unconditional; i.e., no understandings or strings attached. The donee must have the freedom to do with the money as he or she pleases. But some parents make gifts anyway, and some children set the money aside, even though they do not have to.

9. **Pay down the mortgage or make repairs/improvements on the home.** This is a way to convert countable assets (cash) into an exempt asset – the home is exempt, regardless of the amount of equity, if the person lives in the home or intends to return to it. The problem, in the case of single people, is that it probably would not help your heirs or beneficiaries in the long run. You cannot give the home away without incurring a waiting period. Nor can you sell it and remain eligible because the proceeds from the sale would be countable. If the home is neither sold nor given away, that means that it will be in your estate upon your death and be subject to estate recovery or a Medicaid lien. Paying down the mortgage would be most viable for a single applicant if he or she was certain the nursing home stay would only be a few months. But, even then, estate recovery could enter in after death.

10. **Gift to favored family member.** Unlimited amounts of excess countable resources can be given to a minor child (under age 21) or to a blind child (any age) or to a permanently and totally disabled child (any age). In Example 28, the couple gifted their rental house to a disabled child. It would not matter for Medicaid purposes whether the countable asset was investment property or cash because unlimited amounts

can be given to these favored family members. (However, there can be income tax disadvantages associated with gifts. See Example 6).

Spend-down options for married couples. Married couples have all of the options listed above which are available to a single applicant, plus a number of additional options based on the fact that transfers between spouses are not treated as gifts. In addition, the Community Spouse Monthly Income Allowance and Community Spouse Resource Allowance come into play, and, as has been noted, they can sometimes even be increased.

The Community Spouse Resource Allowance is determined as of the time the applicant starts receiving care that lasts for 30 consecutive days. This is the point in time when the "snap shot" is taken – i.e., when resources are tallied up and classified as either exempt or countable. You want the countable assets to be as high as possible on the snap shot date so that the CSRA will be as high as possible. After the snap shot of assets, you can develop a spend-down strategy because the amount is known. Here are some of the more common strategies.

1. Purchase a home or larger home.

EXAMPLE 43.

Spend-down on larger home - Bill and Sue rent an apartment. They had $300,000 in investments on the day continuous care for Bill started. Sue's CSRA would be $95,100, the maximum. The spend-down would be $202,900 ($300,000 -$95,100 -$2,000). Sue buys a home in her name for $210,000. This makes sense because her daughter is coming to live with her anyway. Since the home is exempt, Bill passes the Resource Test and qualifies for Medicaid (assuming, as always, that he also passes the Income Test). After Bill is qualified, Sue can sell the home or borrow against it to raise cash without affecting Bill's eligibility, provided it is in her name.

Note that they should apply for Medicaid before getting a larger home as it will result in a larger CSRA for Sue. If they purchased a $210,000 house before continuous care started, total countable assets would be $90,000 and Sue's CSRA would only be $45,000, as opposed to $95,100 in this example.

2. Put money into existing home.

a. Pay off the mortgage, if any.

EXAMPLE 44.

Paying off the mortgage - This is another example of putting countable resources into an exempt asset. Mr. & Mrs. Mason own their home subject to a $55,000 mortgage, a car and $100,000 in countable assets at the time Mr. Mason needs long-term care. They will have to spend down $48,000 (half of $100,000 less $2,000) before Mr. Mason will qualify for Medicaid. In order to give Mrs. Mason full control over a valuable asset which she will need after his demise, Mr. Mason quitclaims his interest in the home to her. This also avoids estate recovery or Medicaid lien. (If Mr. Mason were not competent, she would use her durable power of attorney to quitclaim his interest, assuming a power of attorney exists and that it sanctions gifts to the agent). Mrs. Mason withdraws $48,000 from savings and pays down the mortgage. Mr. Mason then qualifies for Medicaid. After he is qualified, she can sell the home or refinance it to raise cash. Again, they should apply for Medicaid before paying down the mortgage in order to keep the CSRA as high as possible.

b. Make needed home improvements

New roof or carpeting

New washer, dryer, etc.

Remodel to make home wheelchair accessible

3. Put money into other exempt assets

Purchase a newer car

Purchase medical equipment and supplies

4. Purchase an annuity

Although this strategy has limited application for unmarried applicants, it sometimes works very well for married applicants, particularly where the Community Spouse already has high monthly income. Annuities work because an item is counted either as income or as a resource for purposes of determining eligibility, not both. As long as the payout election cannot be changed and the stream of payments is not assignable, an annuity paying a certain amount per month is in many states treated as income, not an asset. By purchasing a lump-sum, immediate-payout annuity, resources are converted into income. Note, however, that to avoid making a gift to the contingent beneficiaries, the payout period cannot exceed the applicant's life expectancy under the Social Security mortality tables. An 80-year old could not, for instance, buy an annuity with a 20-year payout and direct that the remainder be paid to the children upon her death. Part of the remainder would be an indirect gift to the contingent beneficiaries named in the annuity (because her remaining life expectancy is less than 20 years) and the gift portion would result in a waiting period.

EXAMPLE 45.

Annuity to give CS even higher income - Mr. Johnson needs long-term care. Mr. & Mrs. Johnson own their home, a car and $100,000 in countable assets. They will have to spend down $48,000 (half of $100,000 less $2,000) before Mr. Johnson will qualify for Medicaid. Mrs. Johnson's income is $2,000 per month and Mr. Johnson's income is $350. As you will recall, Mrs. Johnson, the Community Spouse, is not obliged to use her income to support Mr. Johnson; it does not matter how high her income is. So they transfer $48,000 out of their joint account into an account in her name only. This inter-spousal transfer is not treated as a gift. Immediately after the transfer, their countable assets are the same because the assets of both spouses are pooled. Mrs. Johnson purchases a $48,000 annuity, making an irrevocable election to receive payments over the next 5 years. Her life expectancy under the Social Security mortality table is 8 years. The insurance laws in her state give an annuity purchaser a 30-day cooling off period, during which she can change her mind about the investment. Since she could get access to her $48,000, the state Medicaid agency will treat the annuity as an available resource for 30 days. After 30 days, she will no longer be able to cancel the annuity. Her right to the payments cannot be assigned, and there is no way she can get any money from the insurance company, other than the scheduled monthly payments. At this point, a countable asset has been converted to income for Mrs. Johnson, and Mr. Johnson qualifies for Medicaid. The annuity increases her income by several hundred dollars a month without affecting Mr. Johnson's eligibility.

As with almost every other spend-down strategy, it works in some states but not in others. Some states equate an annuity to an irrevocable trust and a few states treat the purchase as a gift, at least to the extent that the amount exceeds the CSRA. Since the laws vary so greatly, competent legal counsel should always be sought before sacrificing such a large portion of one's liquidity for a stream of payments from an insurance company.

Annuities are not always advantageous, as it depends on the incomes of the spouses.

EXAMPLE 46.

Annuity does not help low income CS - In the previous example, if Mrs. Johnson's income were $350 and Mr. Johnson's were $2,000, an annuity would not help her in a meaningful way because she would be entitled to $1,211 from Mr. Johnson's income in order to raise her income to the basic $1,561 support amount (2004-2005 figure). The annuity income would have the effect of reducing the income transfer from Mr. Johnson's Social Security/pension, dollar for dollar. That much more of Mr. Johnson's income would go toward his cost of care.

AVOIDING ESTATE RECOVERY.

The Resource Test, Income Test, spend-down strategy, Community Spouse Resource Allowance and practically everything else discussed to this point pertain to qualifying someone for Medicaid assistance. But there is more to take into consideration. What happens when someone dies? The state Medicaid agency will want to be reimbursed if at all possible. Some state Medicaid agencies have been aggressively engaged in estate recovery for many years, and other states had no recovery program. The Omnibus Budget Reconciliation Act of 1993 (OBRA) mandated that all states adopt programs to recover from the Medicaid recipient's estate for benefits paid after age 55. To the best of the author's knowledge, all states now have estate recovery programs in place, although the scope of the recovery varies widely.

In addition to mandating estate recovery, OBRA gave states the option to expand the scope of estate recovery to include "assets conveyed to a survivor, heir or assign through joint tenancy, life estate, living trust or other arrangement;" i.e., assets that are not subject to probate, but not including life insurance. Many states have expanded their regulations to broaden the scope of estate recovery, and some are even eying life insurance. This expansion of estate recovery has turned long-standing state and common law upside down and turned state Medicaid agencies into claimants with super priority. An ordinary creditor of a decedent, for instance, cannot recover, post-death, out of jointly-owned property or an annuity, since they pass directly to the surviving joint owner or named beneficiary free of creditor claims. But, now, many state Medicaid agencies can recover out of the decedent's assets owned as of his death, up to the amount of assistance rendered. The state can only recover from assets owned by the decedent, so if his name was on title of a rental house with his brother, one half of the value of the property would be susceptible to recovery.

However, a number of restrictions on estate recovery remain which favor the spouse, minor children, blind children, and disabled children. The state cannot recover as long as the deceased Medicaid recipient is survived by one of these favored family members. The claim is held in abeyance and cannot be collected until the surviving spouse dies, or until the minor children attain the age of majority.

Here are some examples to help put the concept of estate recovery into perspective, discussed in terms of saving the family home.

EXAMPLE 47.

Transfer of home to Community Spouse - Kevin needs skilled nursing care and passes both the Income Test and Resource Test. He and his wife own their home as tenants by the entireties or joint with survivorship. If title is left as is, up to one half the value of the home (depending on the amount of Medicaid assistance Kevin received) will probably be subject to estate recovery after Kevin's death.

Now assume that before applying for Medicaid assistance, the home is transferred to his wife. After Kevin qualifies for Medicaid, his wife can sell the home or give it away without affecting Kevin's eligibility. There should be no estate recovery upon Kevin's passing, whether or not she continues to live in it. She can sell it any time she wishes and move to assisted living. She could even give it to the children. The gift will not affect Kevin's eligibility, but it would trigger a waiting period with respect to his wife, equal to the value of the home divided by the gift rate in their state. She would not be eligible until the waiting period, up to 36 months, had expired.

If his wife keeps the home and later needs Medicaid assistance, she would qualify but the home would be exposed to estate recovery for the cost of her care if still in her name.

EXAMPLE 48.

Medicaid lien - Now assume that Kevin's state has Medicaid liens and that title to the home is left in both names. The state Medicaid agency gives the required notice of its intent to record a lien. They do not object or request a hearing, and the lien is recorded. The state Medicaid agency cannot pursue its lien rights as long as Kevin's spouse (or his minor, blind or disabled child) lives in it. After Kevin passes away, his wife can continue to live in the home for the rest of her life. If she decides to sell the house and move to assisted living or spend the money, the state should release its lien – the main purpose of the lien is to protect the state from attempts to give Kevin's half away. After the death of Kevin's wife, the state can recover for the Medicaid assistance rendered to Kevin after age 55 but only out of his half interest in the home.

Caution: These scenarios should hold true in all states, but nothing is guaranteed under Medicaid law! All states have some type of "fraudulent conveyance" law whereby creditors can, within a certain number of years, challenge gifts which made the transferor insolvent. It is an open question as to whether these laws would apply to gifts in the Medicaid context.

EXAMPLE 49.

Estate recovery - Michael, who is single, needed long-term care after his health suddenly failed. His only asset is his home, which is exempt, so he immediately qualified for Medicaid assistance. He passed away four months later. A probate proceeding was required to pay creditors and transfer the home to his heirs or beneficiaries. Even if the state does not have Medicaid liens, the state is a creditor and has a claim for reimbursement in the probate proceeding. In most states the claim is given priority, meaning that it will get paid before general creditors in case the assets are insufficient to pay all creditors. Unless the executor is able to refinance or negotiate a repayment plan, the home will have to be sold to repay the state for Medicaid assistance rendered. State Medicaid agencies will sometimes negotiate a repayment plan with the family but will understandably want interest and the security of a mortgage or trust deed.

EXAMPLE 50.

Sale of home and gift of proceeds - Change the facts slightly and assume that Michael sold the home a few months after he started receiving Medicaid assistance. He was immediately disqualified – the cash from the sale is a countable asset exceeding $2,000. He then made a "half-a-loaf" gift to his children, keeping enough cash to cover his cost of care until the waiting period expired. (If Michael was not competent to do this, his agent under a durable power of attorney could sell the home, provided that the power of attorney authorized the agent to sell it and authorized the gifts.) There is authority in some states that the Medicaid agency should release its lien. And there should be no obligation to repay the state for financial assistance received prior to sale of the home. That is, the state's recovery rights should not become enforceable until his death.

After the waiting period expires and his countable assets drop below $2,000, he re-applies for Medicaid assistance. This strategy, if successful, would not save the home but would save a good portion of the equity. Again, state laws vary because some states in this example would seek recovery of the accumulated lien amount at the time the home is sold. In addition, the state might be able to assert a claim that the gift was a fraudulent conveyance – the state was a creditor at the time of the gift and the gift rendered the Medicaid applicant insolvent. At a minimum, the application would be carefully scrutinized.

It is difficult to know what to do in these situations because no one has a crystal ball. If Michael had Alzheimer's disease but was otherwise in good health, he might live for a number of years. It might make sense to take the rather drastic step of selling the home and making a gift to the children. On the other hand, if his medical condition indicated that his remaining life expectancy is rather short, it might be better to just wait and see what the future holds.

EXAMPLE 51.

Renting the home - Now assume that Michael, clinging to the hope of being able to return, refused to sell his home. After six months it was apparent that Michael would never recover to the point where he would be able to live independently at home. His doctor would not provide a medical certification that Michael would be able to return home. The state Medicaid agency might insist that the home either be sold or rented. Federal law requires that the home be exempt for six months, but the states have different ways of handling it after six months.

If he rented the home, the net rental income would count as income and be applied toward his cost of care. Depending on the circumstances, this might be the preferable option, even though the home will eventually be subject to the Medicaid lien or estate recovery. If it were sold, Michael would have to pay privately and the private pay rate would be higher than the state's contract rate with the nursing home. Leaving title in Michael's name enables the state to recover after his death; but the payback bill will be lower than his private pay bill would have been. And the home might appreciate in value in the meantime.

EXAMPLE 52.

Forced share issue - Here is another variation on estate recovery. Let's assume that Michael is married and that his wife changed her will to leave everything to their children and nothing to Michael. She dies unexpectedly, and her will is probated. The probate laws in their state give the surviving spouse the right to claim a percentage of the deceased spouse's estate, but Michael does not pursue his right, either because he is incompetent or because he will lose his eligibility after recovering the forced share and would rather have it all go to their children. The state Medicaid agency may have the right to pursue estate recovery on Michael's behalf! It presumably could petition to be appointed as the conservator or guardian of Michael's estate and pursue the forced share on Michael's behalf. After the recovery, Michael would lose his eligibility because his countable assets would exceed $2,000. The proceeds recovered will be applied toward his future cost of care, and some states would reimburse themselves at the time of the recovery. As always, the state will have a priority claim for reimbursement at the time of Michael's death, but he might not own much by then.

But note that the state, as conservator, only steps into Michael's shoes; if state law only allowed the forced share to be asserted against probate assets and there were no probate assets (because the deceased spouse owned everything jointly with the children, let's say, or in a living trust), then this strategy would not succeed for the state.

Gift of Home with Retained Life Estate. Someone contemplating a gift of the home should be aware that he or she loses the right to live in the home after the deed has been recorded. He no longer owns it and is at the mercy of the donee. (If there were "understandings" or strings attached to the transfer, of course, it would not be a completed gift!). Even if the donor has full confidence that the child or other donee will "do what's right," there is an inevitable loss in the feeling of security. And there is no guarantee that the child might not get divorced or file for bankruptcy, which could cause major problems.

The examples earlier in this chapter discuss the benefits of transferring the home to the Community Spouse, if there is one. Single people sometimes gift their home to their children and retain a life estate; that is, the lifetime right of use and occupancy. If done properly, the donor/Medicaid recipient would retain the right to live in the home, plus the right to the rental income if he moved to assisted living. In addition, donor's heirs would get a stepped-up basis on the death of the donor; i.e., the tax basis of the children would jump to the full fair market value on the death of the donor. So a gift with a retained life estate would overcome most of the practical disadvantages associated with an outright gift.

Whether it would work for Medicaid purposes is open to question. An ever-increasing number of states are subjecting life estates to estate recovery, making it imperative that someone contemplating a gift of the home with a retained life estate consult an attorney about the specific state law that will apply. Thus, in Example 53 below, if Sandy gifted her home, retained a life estate and later needed Medicaid assistance after the waiting period had expired, a state with regulations to recover out of life estates would assert its right to reimbursement after her death.

A gift with a retained life estate would solve the carry-over basis problem on death but not if the home is sold prior to the donor's death. Look at the adverse tax consequences if the home has to be sold after the gift but prior to the death of the person holding the life estate:

EXAMPLE 53.

Gift of home with retained life estate - It was a priority to Sandy that she leave their home to her children. She was in good health, but was concerned that if she needed long-term care, it would impoverish her. So she gifted the home to her two children and retained a life estate. The life estate continues as long as she is living. It looked like the answer because she can live in the home for the rest of her life or enjoy the benefit of the rental income if she moves to assisted living. She has made a gift, for both Medicaid and tax purposes, equal to the fair market value of their home less any mortgage and less the value of her retained life estate (determined under the Social Security mortality tables based on her age). The advantage to Sandy is that she has the right to continue living there for the rest of her life, even if one of the children dies, gets divorced or files for bankruptcy.

But suppose she is forced to sell the home several years later to raise cash. Let's assume that in the minds of their children, Dick and Jane, the proceeds belong to Sandy. They are cooperative and the sale closes. Sandy purchased the home in 1980 for $100,000 in 1980, and it is now worth $400,000. Dick and Jane are not entitled to the $250,000 capital gains exclusion because they have not lived in the home for two out of the last five years. Furthermore, they took a carry-over basis in the home based on the original $100,000 purchase price in 1980 based on their percentages under the mortality tables, which are assumed here to be 40% at the time of the gift and 55% at the time of the sale. Here are the tax consequences:

	Time of gift	**Time of sale**
Sandy - parent		
% value of life estate	60%	45%
tax basis	$60,000	
% of sale proceeds @ 45%		$180,000
less tax basis		- 60,000
capital gain		$120,000
less $250,000 exclusion		- 250,000
amount of capital gain		0

	Time of gift	Time of sale
Dick & Jane - children		
% value of remainder	40%	55%
tax basis	$40,000	
% of sale proceeds @ 55%		$220,000
less tax basis		- 40,000
amount of capital gain		$180,000

Interestingly, Sandy could continue her life estate in her share of the proceeds. The escrow company closing the sale should be instructed to split the proceeds and to issue separate checks to Sandy and the children. Sandy's proceeds should be kept in a separate account. If the plan was to get a smaller home, the separate account should be paid directly into escrow, and Sandy's new home should be deeded directly to her.

Let's change this scenario slightly and assume that rather than retaining a life estate, Sandy only retained the right to occupy the home, so that if she moved out, her right of occupancy would cease. This is not a life estate because it will not necessarily continue for the remainder of her life. If she later moved out and went to assisted living, her quasi-life estate would cease. Medicaid would probably treat the relinquished interest as a gift, which would trigger a waiting period of up to 36 months. Equally alarming, the children would own a $400,000 home with a very low tax basis.

Strategies to save the family home require a high degree of knowledge of state real property law, tax law, and Medicaid law. It is essential that you get the benefit competent counsel before taking any steps.

TRUSTS.

You may have noticed that very little mention has been made of trusts. That's because, for all practical purposes, trusts have become a liability for purposes of Medicaid planning. The Omnibus Budget Reconciliation

Act of 1993 ("OBRA") essentially eliminated trusts as useful Medicaid planning devices. After OBRA, the consequence of funding an irrevocable trust depends on whose money was used to fund it – the applicant's or someone else's. If the applicant's own funds are used to fund an *irrevocable trust* in which neither the applicant nor spouse has any rights, the transfer will be treated as a gift because an irrevocable trust is an independent entity, a third party. As a result, the transfer will trigger a waiting period the same as any other gift to a third person – the value of the gift divided by the state's gift rate. In addition, due to the 60-month look-back period applicable to trust transactions, the waiting period could be as long as 60 months, making this strategy impractical for most seniors.

In most states transfers to *revocable trusts* are ignored because the trustor can revoke the trust at any time. Assets in revocable trusts are considered available and are treated as either exempt or countable, the same as though there was no trust. In a few states, however, a home owned by a revocable trust loses its exempt character, in which case it must be conveyed out of the trust and back to trustor in order to qualify him for Medicaid assistance. Hopefully, the applicant will still be living in it!

A few types of trusts are still useful under Medicaid law. OBRA 1993 sanctioned "Trusts for a Disabled Persons Under 65." These are special needs trusts for recipients of Medicaid and/or Supplemental Security Income who have acquired a substantial sum of money that would otherwise disqualify him or her from further public assistance. These are usually situations where money is recovered for a personal injury or is inherited, but it would include any windfall. The funds (which belong to the disabled person) are transferred to a trust established by the parent, guardian, grandparent or the court. The funds in such a trust are not regarded as a disqualifying countable asset. But the catch is that, after death, the State gets reimbursed from the remainder of funds in the trust ahead of the heirs or beneficiaries (limited to the amount of public assistance rendered). These trusts are known as "pay back trusts." During his or her lifetime, the Medicaid recipient will have enjoyed distributions from the trust, for things other than food, clothing, and shelter. This would include consumer items such as airline tickets for vacations and visiting relatives, phone service, cable TV, medical procedures not covered by Medicare, and the like. Since the state recovers its outlays before the surviving family members get anything, there is no incentive for the trustee to be stingy on distributions. It makes more sense to spend the funds to enhance the beneficiary's well being. Note that although states are to follow the SSI guidelines in terms of permissible distributions, some states are creating their own rules and they are often much harsher. It is important to seek the guidance of an elder law attorney when considering the creation of a this type of trust.

As mentioned, some states are "income cap" states under Medicaid law. This means that if the applicant's income is over the income maximum, he or she will not qualify for Medicaid assistance. Something has to be done with the excess income. An "income cap" trust (a/k/a Miller trust) is the usual means of dealing with such situations. An income cap trust is an irrevocable trust into which all of the applicant's income is placed. All income gets paid out in a particular priority each month. The remaining funds in the trust at the Medicaid recipient's death are paid to the state. An income cap trust deals only with income and does not represent an opportunity to shelter assets for the family. It is simply a way to qualify an applicant for Medicaid where he would not otherwise qualify due to excess income.

The changes in law made by OBRA 1993 apply only to trusts funded with the Medicaid applicant's own funds. The law did not change with respect to trusts funded by someone else. For example, a parent or grandparent could set up a special needs trust for a disabled adult child or grandchild on Medicaid or SSI. The existence of such a trust, if the trustee was given the proper distribution instructions, would not disqualify the beneficiary for the public assistance programs. It is imperative that the trust agreement contain the proper standard for making distributions. The advice of competent counsel is critical in setting up a trust of this type because the regulations for the various public assistance programs are inconsistent.

PERSPECTIVE ON MEDICAID.

Some of the spend-down strategies discussed in this chapter seem rather drastic to this author, such as investing a large sum in an irrevocable, pay-out annuity or making a large gift. So is a petition for support in order to increase the Community Spouse Monthly Income Allowance or Community Spouse Resource Allowance, due to the high legal fees. It would be an easy matter to run the numbers if you had a crystal ball. But since no one has a crystal ball, it is best to be cautious and not let the tail wag the dog. I have seen situations where the family was intent on minimizing its private-pay nursing home bill and went to extremes only to have the ill spouse pass away in a few weeks. They regretted having spent the money or lost their liquidity.

Proper planning is very important in this area. If your incomes and estates are such that Medicaid assistance would become necessary if your health failed and long-term care was needed, it is critical that a properly-drafted power of attorney be signed while you are fully competent. It should authorize your agent to make unlimited gifts to your spouse, which are often needed to accomplish a Medicaid spend-down. If gifts to your agent are anticipated, the power of attorney should specifically authorize it. Your agent is a fiduciary and cannot make gifts to himself or herself unless the instrument authorizes it.

If a guardianship or conservatorship becomes necessary, the agent under the power of attorney should, to the extent possible, make the Medicaid spend-down transfers before the guardianship or conservatorship is started. A guardian or conservator has different fiduciary duties than an agent under a power of attorney, and a conflict of interest usually arises once the guardianship is commenced.

Medicaid is a very gray area of the law. It will undoubtedly change in the future. There is no guarantee that what might work today will still be viable in several years, when the estate recovery people are looking for ways to recover. The changes are usually more restrictive, and this trend is likely to continue, if not accelerate.

Appendices

When it comes to both lifetime and estate planning, you are relying on surrogates to take care of matters or make decisions when you cannot. They are known in legal parlance as "fiduciaries." The appendices that follow explain the responsibilities and duties applicable to the various fiduciaries discussed throughout this book.

APPENDIX A

FIDUCIARIES IN GENERAL.

Both lifetime plans and estate plans rely heavily on fiduciaries for implementation. You might have served as a fiduciary for someone in the past. Your own estate plan will of necessity rely on one or more fiduciaries, even if you don't have a will or trust! The sections that follow are intended to give you a general understanding of the duties and legal constraints on the various types of fiduciaries.

A fiduciary is someone who serves in a position of trust and confidence. He, she or it manages income and assets for someone else – known as the "beneficiary." The executor or personal representative of the estate of a deceased person is a fiduciary, as is the trustee of a trust. The term "fiduciary" also includes a court-appointed conservator or guardian of the estate of an incompetent person. And it includes the attorney-in-fact (or agent) under a power of attorney and the custodian of a gift to a minor under the Uniform Transfers to Minors Act.

In each instance, the law imposes certain duties on the fiduciary with respect to management of the assets, including the duty of undivided loyalty, duty to invest prudently, duty to delegate prudently, duty not to commingle assets, and to keep records and account. The sections that follow will discuss fiduciary duties in general.

Duty to carry out the duties defined in the instrument. The principal duty of any fiduciary is to carry out the terms of the arrangement. The first place to look in ascertaining those responsibilities is the governing document itself, such as the will, trust agreement, or power of attorney. Hopefully, it will have been thoughtfully drafted and will make the fiduciary's responsibilities clear. A fiduciary is duty-bound to follow any specific instructions, even if he disagrees. Never should action be taken which is contrary to the terms of the governing document. The fiduciary should follow instructions in the instrument, unless, of course, that would require him to violate the law.

Duty of loyalty. Fiduciaries are held to a very high standard of loyalty. A fiduciary cannot put his or her personal interests ahead of those of the estate or trust. For example, assume that a trust agreement directs that the family's summer home be retained as long as possible. You are the trustee and the trust is running out of funds to pay the nursing home costs for the beneficiary, your parent. The summer home must be sold. As a member of the family, you are motivated by a genuine desire to keep the summer home in the family. So you have it appraised and purchase it yourself at the appraised fair market value. This is a breach of the duty of loyalty to the trust! You have a conflict of interest in this situation, even if you paid more than the property was worth. If you want to purchase the summer home, you should get the consent of all beneficiaries or give them notice and get a court order authorizing the transaction.

While the damage to the trust might seem nominal under the circumstances, what if they discovered oil on the property?! Or what if a new freeway came into the area and raised values? The transaction would be "voidable" from the trust's viewpoint. You might later find yourself in the position of having to pay the trust for lost profits, thus making you a guarantor or underwriter of future events beyond your control.

Duty of prudent investment. A fiduciary has a duty to invest as a hypothetical "prudent person" would invest. This requires a fiduciary to put investment assets to productive use as quickly as possible. Checks should be deposited promptly and rental property kept rented. Unless there is a trust agreement or will or other governing document providing to the contrary, unproductive assets should normally be sold and the proceeds invested productively. Speculative investments should be avoided. Note that what seems prudent to you personally might not meet the prudent person standard applicable to fiduciaries. If it is a long-term situation due to a lifetime beneficiary, trust investments should be diversified to get some long-term growth. The lifetime beneficiary will want income investments, and the remaindermen will want long-term growth. The fiduciary has a duty to both. Even the lifetime beneficiary should want long-term growth if he or she is young because inflation is everyone's long-term enemy.

Duty to delegate prudently. Someone had confidence in your ability to manage the trust estate, or you would not have been nominated. That confidence in you, however, does not mean that you have to rely solely on your own judgment in managing the assets. You can delegate to professional advisors, but you must do so prudently and be aware of the costs. You cannot turn the responsibilities over to someone else and be done with it. You are held to the "prudent person" standard both in selecting the advisor and in adopting, monitoring and adjusting a plan of diversification. You should review the background, qualifications and performance record of several potential money managers before discretionary investment authority is delegated. Rating agencies rank the performance of money managers by quartile, so that their performance can be compared with other money managers having similar investment objectives. Even though past performance is no guarantee of similar future results and even though the ranking system itself will always have some flaws, you would not want to select an advisor who had consistently ranked in the third and fourth quartile over the last five years or ten years. And you have a continuing duty to review his or her performance periodically.

Money managers tend to fall into two categories – those who manage for institutions and those who manage for private clients. Institutional money managers tend to gravitate toward a single style, such as small cap, large cap, growth, growth & income, etc. Those who manage for private clients will also diversify in various ways, but they are more likely to have expertise in managing estates having single, large positions with significant capital gains built-in. Maybe the majority of a portfolio is stock in a company that the client previously worked for, or stock in a company that he still owns and operates. In these situations greater diversification is needed, but you cannot sell without incurring a sizeable capital gain liability. If you are faced with this dilemma, be sure to understand the strategies that he or she would be considering.

Most money managers operate on an annual percentage, payable one-fourth each quarter. Trading expenses are extra, but they do not benefit the money manager. If resources are to be invested in mutual funds, you should educate yourself as to the costs, such as commissions, expense ratios, 12b5 charges, and the like. What will the money manager's fees be? What value is the money manager adding? If it is asset allocation (i.e., the mix between bonds and stocks), you might be able to find a total return mutual fund that does the allocation within the fund. I have seen situations where the money manager charges 1% a year and positions the assets in very efficient, no-load mutual funds, with good results. I have also seen situations where people end up paying twice for the same investment advice – the money manager's fee and the mutual fund load – and get marginal results.

The fiduciary will have to decide whether the investment objective is to be income, growth or some combination of both. "Asset allocation" is no more than an attempt to find the right balance between income and growth, and it is by no means a science. The result will depend largely on the direction of the stock market, the direction of interest rates and the value of the dollar on world-wide markets, none of which submit willingly to forecasting. So a money manager should be selected with great care.

Duty not to commingle assets. Fiduciaries are under a strict duty not to commingle assets of the beneficiaries with personal assets. The fiduciary has the burden of proving what is his or hers personally and what belongs to the estate or trust. This makes it vital that good records be kept. Each trust asset should be titled so as to leave no doubt who owns it.

Duty to keep records. The duty of good record keeping is a corollary of the duty not to commingle assets. If you fail to keep good records, you might not be able to prove what is yours and what is the estate's. If personal investments are not segregated from investments of the estate or trust, losses might be presumed to be yours and gains presumed to belong to the trust or estate. If you are the trustor setting up the trust, a good accounting system should be established at the outset for maintaining a record of assets owned by the trust and the tax basis of each. If you are a successor trustee, set up a record-keeping system when you accept the responsibility so that cash receipts and distributions can be easily memorialized. You will also want a record-keeping system that will enable you to distinguish between receipts that are income and receipts that are principal.

If you are called upon to serve as successor trustee or executor of an estate, you should immediately apply for a tax identification number (IRS form SS-4) if one does not already exist and open a bank account in the name of the trust or estate.

Duty to provide information. A fiduciary has a duty in general to provide information to the beneficiaries. An executor or conservator is usually required to render an annual accounting of receipts and expenditures. A final report to the court is also due when the estate is closed. Even if accountings are not required under state law or the terms of the governing instrument, it would be good practice to give an annual accounting to the beneficiaries anyway. Misgivings are always quicker to arise when full disclosure is not made. An accounting will keep them informed and dispel any later argument that they were kept in the dark while you were making allegedly bad management decisions.

Hidden risks for a fiduciary. Before you accept an appointment as fiduciary, you should make sure that the estate does not own any real property which might have been contaminated with hazardous substances, as defined by the Environmental Protection Agency or the state equivalent. You might find yourself saddled with personal liability merely by stepping into the role, even though the contamination occurred years earlier. If you have any doubts, get an environmental assessment before accepting. Cleanup is ghastly expensive, even for something as simple as an old fuel oil tank which is no longer used but which leaks.

Should you agree to serve as fiduciary? If you are nominated to act as fiduciary, ask yourself whether you want to serve? Do you have the time and patience? The temperament? Is there someone who is closer or better situated to carry out the responsibilities? Sometimes, the responsibilities are minimal – e.g., custodian of a minor's account. At other times, the responsibilities can seem endless – e.g., the conservator or executor of an estate of which nothing is known and where there are "vultures" lurking in the shadows, meaning people who want things they are not entitled to. The role as a fiduciary is not one that should be accepted without thought. If there is some major impediment to your serving, it might be better not to accept the appointment.

APPENDIX B

EXECUTOR.

When someone dies owning assets in his or her name that must be probated, the court appoints a fiduciary known as the executor to handle the administration of the estate. In some states, the person named in a will is referred to as an "executor" ("executrix" = feminine) or an "administrator" or "personal representative" or "personal administrator" ("administratrix" = feminine) if there is no will. In other states, all such fiduciaries, with or without a will, are generically referred to as "personal representatives." For convenience and consistency, the person appointed by the court to handle the administration of a deceased person's estate is usually referred to as an "executor," regardless of whether there was a will or not. The responsibilities are essentially the same for both.

The role of this fiduciary in general terms is to identify, gather and value the assets; to pay valid claims and debts and reject invalid claims; to prepare final tax returns; and to distribute the remaining assets pursuant to the terms of the will (or laws of intestate succession). In some cases very little is involved in serving as executor; in other cases much is required, and it can be a major and protracted undertaking.

Who will be appointed as executor? If the deceased person left a valid will, the person nominated in the will is normally appointed by the court to serve as executor, unless he or she is under the legal age, is of unsound mind or has been convicted of some disqualifying criminal offense. Although some people nominate a bank, trust company or other corporate fiduciary to act as executor, most people will nominate their spouse, a relative or a trusted friend to serve in that capacity.

If the decedent died without a will or if the person nominated in the will declines to act or is disqualified for some reason, the court will appoint an executor according to the priorities set forth in the probate code. The order of priority varies somewhat from state to state but generally is as follows: nominee in the will, if any; spouse; children; parents; siblings; a creditor; state department of revenue.

Duties of the Executor. Once appointed by the court and qualified, the general responsibilities of the executor are as follows:

1. To give notice of his or her appointment and the pendency of the probate. This notice is mailed to the beneficiaries named in the will and to the deceased person's heirs at law - i.e., those who would inherit if there were no will. Notice to creditors must be published in the newspaper.

2. To identify, safeguard, inventory and value the assets of the estate.

3. To identify and notify creditors of the estate and pay valid claims, including income and estate taxes. And to reject claims that are not valid.

4. To distribute what remains according to the terms of the will (or according to the law of intestate succession if there is no will).

5. To account to the court and beneficiaries for assets of the estate, cash received and cash disbursed.

As you can see, the duties of the executor extend in several directions. He or she has a duty to the deceased person to carry out the terms of the will. And a duty to the beneficiaries to protect their interests. And a duty to the creditors to identify them, give notice and pay valid claims.

Sometimes the executor's duties are in conflict. If, for example, the executor pays a creditor's claim which is not valid or which is presented after expiration of the creditors' claim period because it only seems "fair," he may have breached his duty to the beneficiaries. On the other hand, if the executor fails to conduct a diligent search for names and addresses of creditors in the hope that fewer claims against the estate will be presented, the duty to the creditors will have been breached.

Steps to take upon appointment. Upon being appointed executor and taking any further steps that might be required to qualify, such as filing an oath or bond, the executor should get several certified copies of the "letters." The clerk of the court will issue "letters testamentary" (will) or "letters of administration" (no will). The letters are the executor's badge of authority, so to speak, informing third parties such as banks, brokerage firms, and title companies that executor is authorized to act on behalf of the estate. There should be no problems in dealing with the financial institutions after presenting certified copies of the letters. Several certified copies of the "letters" might be needed, depending on the number and types of accounts and assets in the estate. Some institutions will insist on a certified copy for their files, and others will be content with taking a photocopy of your certified copy, which will save the estate the cost of the certified copy. The probate court will issue more certified copies if later needed.

The executor should apply for a Employer Identification Number (EIN) for the estate promptly after qualifying. This is a simple matter of filling out IRS Form SS-4 and mailing or "FAXing" it to the Internal Revenue Service. An EIN can also be obtained online at www.irs.gov. A tax number will be issued with little delay and with that number, you will be able to open a bank account in the name of the estate. Don't be tempted to use your personal Social Security Number to open the account because then the interest would appear on a 1099 in your name. Wait until the estate gets its own EIN.

Protecting Assets. The executor's first order of business after appointment should be to secure and safeguard the assets of the estate. Is there is any possibility that some of the heirs might be tempted to "help themselves?" To guard against disappearance, the executor should take physical possession of valuable personal property, such as valuable art objects, jewelry, furs, and coin collections, immediately after letters of administration or letters testamentary are received. Depending on the family dynamics, door locks maybe should be changed to deny access to unauthorized persons. The executor is also obligated to make sure the home and any other improved real property are insured against casualty losses and theft. Unreasonable delay in so doing could subject a well-meaning executor to personal liability for losses suffered by the estate after his or her appointment.

If the decedent operated a business, get professional counsel to decide what steps should be taken.

Inventory safety deposit box. Access to the deceased person's safety deposit box should be sought. Banks are fairly cooperative in allowing a search for a will before a probate is opened but will be reluctant to release the will or any other contents without proof of authority to act on behalf of the estate; i.e., "letters." The degree of red tape to get access varies widely, ranging from simply presenting a certified copy of your letters to getting a court order. States having an inheritance tax might require the presence of a bank employee or agent from the department of revenue when the box is opened and inventoried. Even if not required, it is good practice to have a third party present when the box is opened and an inventory taken – it places the executor's conduct above question by disgruntled heirs.

Notifying third parties. Interested third parties should be promptly notified of the person's death. Unless the executor lives in the decedent's residence, the U.S. Post Office should be notified so that the decedent's mail can be forwarded to the executor. The Post Office will require a certified copy of the letters testamentary or letters of administration plus a completed address-forwarding card. It is essential that the executor review incoming mail, both for evidence of unknown assets and for the existence of creditors. At some point during the administration of the estate, the executor will have to give notice to known creditors.

The Social Security Administration should be notified of the death and request made for the burial allowance. Any third parties sending monthly pension or annuity checks should be notified. If the decedent was a veteran, the state and/or federal Veterans Administration should be contacted, as there may be death benefits payable or payments to stop. If the person died near the end of the month, his or her Social Security and pension check for the next month will probably be automatically deposited to the checking account and have to be refunded. Leave the checking account open, and the Social Security Administration will automatically retrieve the payment and save you the trouble.

Newspaper and magazine subscriptions should be cancelled and refunds obtained where possible. Utility companies should be notified, future bills sent in the name of the estate or the service cancelled and refunds of any deposits obtained. Credit card companies should be promptly notified of the death and the cards cancelled, particularly if care givers or relatives might have been using them. Be sure to ask whether there was any credit life insurance. Any mortgage company should be notified and inquiry made as to whether there was any mortgage life insurance.

The decedent's employer or past employer should be contacted. If the deceased person was employed at the time of death, there may be final compensation, bonuses or vacation pay to be collected. If the decedent was retired, there might nevertheless be life insurance, pension or profit sharing plans, stock options or death benefits of some type.

There is no easy answer if you think an insurance policy or annuity exists but can't find it in the safe deposit box or personal belongings. You may know from comments made by the decedent which company may have issued a policy. Contact the decedent's employer, former employer or union. Contact its local agent or go to the company's website. Look at last year's tax return for possible interest earnings, look through the decedent's checking account records for evidence of premium payments or receipts of cash.

Notifying brokerage firms. Brokerage firms should be notified of the decedent's passing. Upon being notified of an account owner's passing, the brokerage firm will handle the account as described on page 33:

Documentation such as certified copy of death certificate; certified copy of letters testamentary or letters of administration; affidavit of domicile (form probably provided by brokerage firm); and signed stock power(s) to transfer the securities to the new owner(s) will be required. In some cases, they will also want estate and inheritance tax releases. If the account contains mutual funds or limited partnerships in addition to stocks and bonds, additional copies of the death certificate and letters will be needed.

U.S. Savings Bonds. U.S. Savings Bonds are unique in that they are not subject to probate. Title passes to the co-owner according to the method of registration under Treasury Regulations. The successor owner must present proof of death of the prior owner. If a successor owner was not named, the bonds would be payable to the owner's estate.

Examining records. The executor must review the decedent's personal financial records with a view to locating assets, identifying creditors and later preparation of tax returns. In addition to incoming mail discussed above, prior tax returns, bank statements and cancelled checks should be scrutinized. If you do not know which CPA or Enrolled Agent prepared the decedent's returns, copies of the decedent's past tax returns can be obtained for a nominal cost by submitting Form 4506 to the Internal Revenue Service. The last three tax years should suffice. The same should be done with the state department of revenue if a state income tax is involved.

In addition to information about earned income on the W-2s, the decedent's prior tax returns will reveal information about possible assets. Schedule B will show interest and dividend income. There is no assurance that the accounts, stocks or bonds still exist, but inquiry should be made. If the last return includes a Form 6252 (Installment Sale Income), there may be a note, trust deed or real estate contract somewhere. Form 6252 will also reflect the percentage of receipts excluded from taxable income as return of capital. This tidbit of information will be needed when the final income tax return for the decedent (Form 1040) and the estate income tax return (Form 1041) are filed. If the decedent itemized deductions, Schedule A will reveal amounts paid for real estate taxes, another indicator of a possible asset.

The customer service departments of title insurance companies are very helpful in identifying real property which the decedent owned. Land records are computerized, and the title company can usually check on ownership of a specific parcel. It can also check the tax assessor's rolls for names and addresses of people who own property or receiving a tax statement.

The bank statements and cancelled checks will provide additional details on sources of payments and possible creditors. You can request microfiche copies of cancelled checks or deposits if additional information is needed.

The records search may produce life insurance policies. The estate is not normally the named beneficiary (the proceeds are exposed to creditors' claims), so find out who the beneficiary is and have them contact the insurance company to collect the policy proceeds.

Investment Decisions. An executor should invest with safety utmost in mind, as his role is limited in time and scope. Unless some of the assets will later be transferred to a trust or the will directs that specific assets be distributed directly to beneficiaries, the executor may want to liquidate stocks and bonds and hold the funds in short-term certificates of deposit or a money market account. The stock market can drop at any time; and if interest rates were to rise, the value of the bonds would fall.

In large estates the account balances should be kept under the limits of insurability of the Securities Investor Protection Corporation ($500,000, no more than $100,000 of which can be cash). Set up another account or an account at another brokerage firm if the balance exceeds SIPC limits.

SAMPLE ATTORNEY'S LETTER TO NEW EXECUTOR.

Note: The time periods referenced in this form letter will differ from one state to the next!

Dear Client:

This is the letter that I give new executors to help them understand their responsibilities and get off to a good start. Not everything will apply to this estate, but the basic responsibilities are basically the same for all executors.

In simplest terms, your role as executor will be to identify, gather and safeguard the assets and income of the estate; to notify beneficiaries, heirs at law and creditors of the proceeding; to pay the costs of administering the estate, debts and any taxes that may be due. After this has been done and the estate is ready to close, what remains will be distributed to the proper heirs or beneficiaries.

Here is the general order in which things will proceed. We will help, so don't feel overwhelmed!

1. We file the petition to get you appointed as executor. Unless there is a will which waives the bond requirement, the court will probably require a bond. If so, you will have to go to an insurance agency which handles bonds, such as _____, It will take a few days to get the bond issued, and it will then have to be filed with by the court.

2. After the bond is accepted by the court, you will be qualified as executor. The court clerk will issue either "letters testamentary" (will) or "letters of administration" (no will). Banks, stock brokers and title companies will all recognize your letters as your badge of authority to act on

behalf of the estate and give you access to funds, safety deposit box, etc. You may need more than one certified copy of your letters; we can get more later if needed.

3. As soon as you are qualified, notice to creditors has to be published once a week for _____ weeks. This starts the ___-month creditors' claim period. We will take care of publication.

4. It is your responsibility to safeguard estate assets. Make sure that the home is covered by casualty insurance. If insurance does not exist, you should take out coverage immediately. If, for example, the home were not insured and happened to burn while you are executor, you could possibly be held personally liable for the loss! In addition, if relatives or friends are accustomed to coming and going from the home, it is normally advisable to change the locks, again to protect yourself. These are all expenses of the estate, so keep your receipts for later reimbursement.

5. We will apply for a federal employee identification number for the estate. This will require a copy of letters of administration. The IRS will assign a tax number in a few days.

6. After receiving the tax number, you should immediately open a bank account in the name of the estate. Make sure it is the type of account where the canceled checks are returned to you and be sure to keep the monthly statements. If you cannot find such an account, get one that mails photocopies of the front and back of canceled checks. Opening a bank account will require another copy of letters of administration, although the bank will often be satisfied by taking a photocopy of your original. *All cash received should be deposited in the bank account and all*

expenditures should be by check out of this bank account. Keep a copy of the receipts and invoices to document the expenditures.

7. Keeping good records of cash receipts and disbursements is one of a executor's most important responsibilities. All funds of the estate should be deposited to the estate account, and all bills paid and distributions should be made out of this account. Keep the monthly statements and canceled checks as they will be needed when we do the final accounting upon closing the estate. Each creditor filing a claim should sign a receipt acknowledging the amount received — we will provide you with a form of Receipt.

8. If the decedent had substantial assets in a stock brokerage account, annuities, mutual funds, etc. and you want to leave them there for the time being, you can take a copy of your letters of administration or letters testamentary (and the estate tax number) to the institution and have them transfer the investments into an account in the name of the estate. If the estate is going to be liquidated and the assets distributed after completion of administration, you might want to have the stocks and bonds sold at this time. My advice is not to play the role of market timer. The market might be going down in the case of stocks or interest rates going up in the case of bonds, either of which could subject you to unwanted criticism.

9. You should also go to the post office and have the decedent's mail forwarded to you. This will alert you to possible creditors and unknown assets. This will require another original of letters of administration.

10. The next major deadline will be the filing of an Inventory, which is a list of all the assets of the estate. This is due ____ days after your ap-

pointment. You should start locating and valuing assets of the estate as soon as possible, starting with the balances in the decedent's bank and stock accounts on the date of death. Other assets may come to light as you get more information. It's always a good idea to review the latest tax returns as they might lead to other assets of which we are not aware. You can get information regarding real property from the tax assessor's office or the title company. You are responsible only for assets which are subject to court jurisdiction/probate. Unless the estate was named as beneficiary, you are not responsible for assets that are transferred by beneficiary designation, such as IRAs, joint accounts, annuities, life insurance and the like. These assets are not subject to administration and do not have to be listed on the Inventory. However, you will want to assist in locating all assets of every nature and make sure that life insurance policies, for instance, are given to the named beneficiary.

11. You should start a list of creditors as they become known to you. Since we do not know how many there are or the total amount, don't pay any until after the creditors' ___ month claim period has expired. There are different classes of creditors and some have priority over others in case there is not enough to go around. Which we hope will not be the case! Check with me on any you are not sure about, as we can reject those that look too high or are in doubt.

12. Lastly, if the estate owns real property and an appraisal will be needed for estate or inheritance tax purposes, find an appraiser right away. We would like to be involved because the appraiser's qualifications have to be included in the appraisal. If the estate is not taxable, it would nevertheless be a good idea to establish the value of the home for capital gains tax purposes. If the property is not sold until years later, you will, at

a minimum, want an opinion letter from a real estate broker stating the value at the date of death.

We will help you as needed in fulfilling these various responsibilities — call anytime you have a question. You may want to hire the decedent's former tax return preparer for help on the tax returns, which will be an expense of the estate. A final individual income tax return will be due for income up until the time of his or her death, and a return will be due for his estate up until the time the assets are distributed.

Very truly yours,

APPENDIX C

TRUSTEE OF A TRUST.

The responsibilities of the trustee of a trust could be very similar to those of an executor of a will, or they might extend over a longer period of time and be more involved. If a friend or relative established a revocable living trust and served as trustee until death and the terms of the trust direct that it is to terminate, then the successor trustee serves in essentially the same role as the executor of a will. Except that there will be no court supervision. This appendix is devoted primarily to longer term trusts.

If the purpose of the trust is such that it will continue for an extended period of time, the trustee will invest differently than he would for the short term. The trustee also might have to exercise discretion in making distributions. A trust that extends over a longer period of time normally involves both income beneficiaries and "remaindermen," to whom the remaining assets will be distributed when the income interest terminates. Sometimes the identity of all the beneficiaries is not even known, but their interests must nevertheless be protected.

The interests of the remaindermen are often at odds with the interests of the income beneficiaries. The income beneficiaries want high income, the remaindermen want high growth, and the objectives are inherently conflicting. For example, if the trust assets are invested in long-term bonds, the income beneficiaries will be pleased with the high yields. But not the remaindermen, as there will be little growth in value to protect their interests from the effects of inflation. With only 3% inflation, the purchasing power of the remaindermen's interest would diminish by 35% in 15 years!

A similar conflict arises if the trustee has discretion to invade the principal of the trust to help an income beneficiary in time of need – there will be less principal left for the remaindermen. These are two common examples of the conflicting interests a trustee is frequently called upon to balance.

Accounting. Because the trustee must distinguish between the income beneficiaries and the remaindermen (who essentially "own" the trust assets but do not get possession until later), proper accounting is very important. The trustee should set up an accounting system that allows receipts and disbursements to be split between principal and income. The accounting system should be maintained in such a way that the amount accruing to each beneficiary can be determined at any point in time.

The trust agreement may address the question of what is principal and what is income. If it does not, the state in question has probably adopted the Uniform Principal and Income Act, under which interest, dividends (except stock dividends and splits), rents, ordinary repairs and one-half the trustee's fees are treated as income items. Proceeds from the sale of trust assets, insurance proceeds from casualty losses, loan repayments, repairs of a capital nature, capital gains taxes and half of the trustee's fee are capital items.

Since professional fees are a trust expense and not the trustee's personal expense, the advice of a CPA should be sought both in setting up the accounting system and in preparing the annual tax return(s). It is well worth the money to get the proper accounting system set up when you start as trustee than to struggle with it at a later time when you cannot remember the details. In addition, depreciation under principal-and-income accounting is a special item which will require the advice of a professional.

Investment decisions. In the absence of a contrary directive in the trust agreement, a trustee will want to diversify and invest some of the portfolio in bonds, some in stocks and leave some in cash. His role is longer term than that of an executor and includes a duty to minimize risk of loss and maximize total return. Studies show that overall risk is diminished and total return (i.e., the total of interest, dividends and capital appreciation) is enhanced if part of the portfolio is invested in bonds and part in stock. Stocks have historically provided a better rate of return than bonds and act as a hedge against inflation, which will please the remaindermen. Meanwhile, the bonds will be adding income to the account in good times and bad.

The trustee should be conservative in choice of investments, sticking with high quality bonds and stocks. If the trustee invested in securities with a high risk/high reward profile and the strategy went awry, the natural tendency will be to judge with 20-20 hindsight. Since there is no clear-cut line between speculation and prudent investment, a fiduciary should err on the conservative side.

APPENDIX D

AGENT UNDER DURABLE POWER OF ATTORNEY.

What is a power of attorney? A power of attorney is a written instrument under which you (the principal) designate someone else (your agent) to act of your behalf. The agent is subject to the general fiduciary duties imposed on all fiduciaries as discussed in Appendix A. The principal can limit the authority of the agent to specific decisions; or, the agent can be authorized to do anything the principal could do. The agent must be expressly authorized to make gifts. The agency relationship could also be limited to a particular period of time and contain an expiration date. Powers of attorney terminate upon the death of the principal.

What is a "durable" power of attorney? Unless state law provides otherwise, an ordinary power of attorney terminates if the principal becomes incompetent. But by adding "durable" provisions to govern if you become incompetent, a power of attorney will remain (or become) valid after incompetency and can be very useful in specific transactions. It will often avoid the need for a formal conservatorship proceeding.

In one of two ways, a durable power of attorney will empower your agent to make decisions after your incompetency. Either the document will provide that "this instrument shall not be affected by my subsequent disability," or words to that effect. Or, it will provide that "this power of attorney shall become effective upon my incompetency." The former version is effective when executed. The latter, sometimes referred to as a "springing" power of attorney, does not become effective until you become incompetent. A mechanism of some type is required in a springing power of attorney to satisfy third parties that you are in fact incompetent and that your agent is authorized to act. A letter from your physician or some other trusted person is commonly used, but there are myriad reports of problems getting financial institutions to honor the power of attorney. They often want additional assurance that the principal is in fact incompetent. With a springing power of attorney it is the fact of incompetency which empowers the agent to make decisions on your behalf. So the document should contain an understandable and objective definition of "incompetency," such as a letter from your physician. This reluctance is easier to overcome if the bank's own power-of-attorney form has previously been signed. The unwillingness of some financial institutions to honor powers of attorney has led to legislation in numerous states which puts some risk on the institution for refusing to honor one.

A power of attorney which "survives" your incompetency is effective from the time of signing, so your agent is authorized to act from the very beginning. This may make it more readily accepted by financial institutions but has the disadvantage in some situations of requiring that the instrument be safeguarded until need for its use arises. (The agent needs the original to do business). Only the most trusted person should be named as your attorney-in-fact under a power of attorney. Even then, caution should be exercised in the custody of such a powerful document.

The flexibility of durable powers of attorney. Powers of attorney are commonly used to convey real estate; the power is recorded first, then the deed or mortgage. Once recorded, it will remain in effect until another instrument is recorded which revokes the original power of attorney (or until it expires by its terms or the principal passes away).

Everyone should have a durable power of attorney, regardless of age, particularly if a more comprehensive solution to possible incapacity does not exist. Any competent person of legal age can execute a power of attorney; but once you become incompetent, it's too late. If need ever arises to sell or re-title assets after incompetency, a durable power of attorney can avoid the need for a conservatorship. It can be drafted to suit your specific situation, such as authorizing your agent to continue a pattern of making gifts to children or grandchildren, or prohibiting gifts.

If you are reluctant to set up and fund a living trust until necessary, your agent under a durable power of attorney can be directed to fund a trust agreement (which should be drafted and incorporated by reference). But the main value of a durable power of attorney is that it allows assets to be sold or mortgaged in order to deal with a changed financial situation – without it, a conservatorship is likely to be needed. Note that special provisions should be included in your durable power of attorney if application for Medicaid would be a possibility in the event of long term care. A durable power of attorney should authorize unlimited gifts between the spouses to facilitate a Medicaid spend-down.

In many states, the durable power of attorney can also be used to nominate a guardian or conservator in the event one is needed. Why might a conservatorship be necessary if your agent already can act under the durable power of attorney? For one thing, a power of attorney only empowers someone else to act on your behalf. It does not deprive you, the principal, of the ability to act. Due to lack of judgment and cognitive ability, seniors can be vulnerable to get rich quick pitches. I have seen situations where the agent was unable to prevent the principal from "giving away the ranch." If it becomes necessary to start a guardianship or conservatorship proceeding, at least you will have named the person of your choice to serve.

The shortcomings of powers of attorney. One distinct disadvantage of a power of attorney is that it is not self-enforcing. Yes, the agent is under a duty of loyalty and is obligated to account to the principal. And the principal can revoke the power of attorney, with or without cause. But we are assuming that the person is relying on the agent due to diminished capacity. What if someone is incompetent, and the agent refuses to account to anyone? Let's assume that the agent transferred funds to a new joint account with himself as the other joint owner. He is paying the bills properly but now refuses to account to anyone. It is usually the agent who refuses to account who has designs on the estate. I have seen these situations arise, and establishment of a conservatorship or litigation may be the only solution.

Durable powers of attorney vs. living trusts. A durable power of attorney accomplishes some of the same objectives with respect to possible disability as a living trust, but the trust is usually preferable. The power of attorney is more appropriate for specific transactions or situations of limited duration. A trust offers a better and more comprehensive solution for dealing with the challenges of incapacity. With an estate having substantial income and assets, management decisions will arise from time to time. It is better to formulate your goals and give your fiduciary guidance via comprehensive instructions in a trust agreement than to rely on a durable power of attorney, which typically contains few standards and little guidance for making investment decisions.

APPENDIX E

DUTIES OF A CONSERVATOR.

A conservator, also known as "guardian of the estate," is a court-appointed fiduciary who is responsible for managing the assets of a minor child or an incompetent adult. These are usually situations where a minor acquires assets by inheritance or personal injury recovery or where an adult has lost his or her ability to manage finances. In some states a conservator is referred to as the "guardian of the estate" to distinguish the role from "guardian of the person." The former handles income and assets and, as discussed in the Appendix F, a guardian makes decisions personal to the protected person.

The role of the conservator is to take charge of the financial affairs of the protected person (or "ward," as he or she has traditionally been known), to deposit funds received and to pay bills. The court usually requires a probate bond to protect the estate against misappropriation by the conservator. The conservator is required to render a full accounting to the court, usually on an annual basis and when the proceeding is closed. The duties of a conservator are similar to those of a trustee under a trust, but a trustee acts under a formal trust agreement and does not report to the court.

It is fairly expensive to establish and maintain a conservatorship. A petition must be filed with the court and notice given to the prospective ward. State statutes commonly provide for the appointment of a "visitor" or guardian ad litem to interview the prospective ward and render a report to the court on the ward's competence (or degree of incompetence). If someone objects, a hearing may be needed. Some state statutes provide for the appointment of an attorney for the prospective ward before the question of incompetency is ruled on. The more people involved, of course, the greater the cost. But the advantage is that the ward's interests will probably be protected better.

The definition of "incompetence" differs by state. In most states, the statute requires that the person be deprived of no more of his or her liberties than necessary to deal with the situation, and the court order should be so limited. But this may not happen unless a hearing is demanded. If no one takes the initiative, an adjudication of total incompetency may result.

Initiating a conservatorship proceeding is a very serious move, quite aside from the expense, as it can have a deleterious effect on a person's emotional well being. In the case of an elderly person who is not getting along so well, less drastic measures should be used to deal with the situation whenever possible. Automatic deposit of pension and Social Security checks and automatic payment of bills wherever possible will help in some situations. Sufficient flexibility can often be attained through use of a joint checking account where a trusted friend or relative can pay the other bills, although funds in such an account should be no more than necessary to handle monthly living costs. A durable power of attorney will avoid the need for a conservatorship in many situations, but again, it will not prevent a gullible person from giving away his assets, as a conservatorship would. When other options fall short and there is no durable power of attorney or living trust, a conservatorship may be the only option.

SAMPLE ATTORNEY'S LETTER TO CONSERVATOR.

Dear Client:

As a conservator, you are a fiduciary who is responsible for identifying, gathering and safeguarding the assets of the protected person. You are responsible for paying his or her bills (including estimated taxes if applicable) and accounting for all estate funds which you receive or pay out. You will be required to account to the court at least annually for all receipts and expenditures. It is very important that you keep detailed and accurate records of account as you go, so that less of our time will be required to prepare the report.

You are also obligated to take possession of and safeguard his or her will. If you find one, let us know and we will place it in safekeeping.

HANDLING OF FUNDS.

Checking Account. The first thing to do after the court issues your "letters of conservatorship" is to open a new bank account in "Your Name, Conservator, Estate of _____" The Social Security number of the protected person is used on the account, so that all interest income and dividends get reported in his or her name, not yours. You can use any bank you wish, but *be sure to open the type of account that mails canceled checks with the monthly statement* – you need to keep the canceled checks for your records. If the bank no longer sends canceled checks, at least be sure you will get photocopies of the fronts and backs of the canceled checks. Close out all existing accounts and deposit the funds in the new estate account. To make the accountings easier, keep the number of accounts to a minimum. If you think more than one account will be necessary, kindly discuss it with us.

All income should be deposited or directed to the conservatorship account, and the account should be used to pay all bills. Only you, the conservator, are allowed to sign. Not even the attorney is authorized to withdraw funds from the estate account. Get as much set up on automatic deposit and automatic withdrawal as possible — it's easier in the long run.

DEPOSITS.

The more information contained in the check register, the easier it will be to prepare the annual report for the court. Make a notation as to what each deposit is for at the time it is made; this saves the time required later to figure out what the deposits were for.

Make note of any *automatic deposits* going into the account each month. This could include pension checks, contract payments coming from a title company, Social Security payments, annuity payments, etc.

WRITING CHECKS.

Printed, numbered checks with both your name and the name of the conservatorship estate should be ordered when the account is opened. Each check written should be recorded in the register at the time it is written as to date, amount, name of payee and a brief notation as to the purpose. You should receive an invoice, statement or receipt of some type and write the check number on the receipt. Keep the receipts.

Again, make note of any *automatic withdrawals* from the account for needs such as insurance premiums, escrow payments, bank service charges, etc. If the amount is not known until the monthly statement is received, make an entry and fill in the amount when the statement arrives. Do as much as possible as you go, which will make the annual account easier and minimize legal expenses.

RECONCILING THE BANK ACCOUNT.

You should reconcile the check register every month. *It should balance to the penny.* If you cannot get it to balance, the bank might be willing to help; or you can call this office. It is far simpler to deal with reconciliation problems each month than to let them build up because after a year, one's memory tends to fail! If you have a computer, you might want to get a program such as Quicken or Quick Books as they make reconciliation so easy. They will also print out a summary of receipts and expenditures to submit to the court with the annual account.

RECORD KEEPING.

Be sure to keep all bank statements and canceled checks because they have to be retained until the conservatorship is closed and your final account filed with the court. You also need to keep invoices and receipts to document expenditures.

INVENTORY AND PRESERVATION OF ASSETS.

Inventory of Assets. A complete inventory of all assets of the estate must be filed with the court within ____days of your appointment. We will prepare the inventory based on the information which you provide. You should start at once preparing a list of assets, including account numbers and balances as of your appointment. Do the best you can at this point; we can amend the inventory later if more assets are found. The Inventory is a very important document as it becomes the starting point for preparing the annual account to the court.

Unless you are sure you can identify all the assets, you should review the protected person's *income tax returns* for the past 2 or 3 years as they will contain 1099s or reference accounts and assets of which you might not be aware. You would also want to review the bank statements for at least the last year as it may indicate other assets or gifts or questionable payments of money. If more assets are discovered later, a Supplemental Inventory must be filed with the court.

If you run across documentation indicating the original cost or tax basis of any of the assets, such as the home or stocks and bonds, keep it for future reference. This information will be needed in the event you have to sell assets to raise cash, in which case capital gains will have to be reported on the income tax return the same as though the protected person had made the sale personally.

If the estate owns real property or valuable personal property, make certain that casualty insurance exists and have your name as conservator added to the policy. If you cannot find a policy, consider taking out casualty insurance – the last thing you want for having agreed to help the protected person is an allegation by one of his or her heirs that you should have insured a home that burned. You could be held personally liable! If the protected person was forgetful about paying bills, check with the county treasurer to make certain that real estate taxes are not in arrears.

Valuable assets, such as coin collections, art, antiques, etc., should be kept in a secure place. They should be itemized and appraised so that no one can later claim that you mishandled them.

WILL AND ESTATE PLAN.

Although neither you nor the court can change the estate plan of the protected person, you are nevertheless obligated to *locate and safeguard any will that he or she may have executed.*

Very truly yours,

APPENDIX F

GUARDIAN.

The term "guardian," or "guardian of the person" in some states, refers to someone who, like the conservator, is appointed by the court. However, the guardian does not handle income and assets. His or her role is limited to making personal decisions, such as where the person is to live and what kind of medical care the protected person is to receive. In the case of minors, the responsibilities also extend to schooling and religious upbringing.

The court could and often does appoint the same person to act as both guardian and conservator. Although a guardian must act in the best interests of the ward, he is not a fiduciary in the same sense as the other fiduciaries discussed above. State statutes usually define the guardian's authority and deny authority to make certain decisions, such as abortion and sterilization.

APPENDIX G

OTHER FIDUCIARIES.

Living Wills and Health Care Agents. A living will does not involve the appointment of another person to act on your behalf – it is a directive to your physician. With a health care power of attorney, however, you appoint someone to make end-of-life medical decisions under circumstances where you cannot. This person is a fiduciary in the sense that he or she must be faithful to your wishes but does not handle finances or money.

Custodian under the Uniform Transfers to Minors Act. All states have adopted some version of the Uniform Transfers to Minors Act or its predecessor, the Uniform Gifts to Minors Act. Gifts to minors made pursuant to these statutes qualify for the $11,000 annual exclusion for gift tax purposes. The donor transfers the funds or asset to a custodian, which could be the donor, a parent, or someone else. The custodian is essentially a trustee operating under the Uniform act, and the minor is the beneficiary. When the minor reaches the specified age (varies from 18 to 25, depending on the state), the assets are distributed to him or her. A separate custodial account must be set up for each child. The accounts are owned under the minor's Social Security number. Since the arrangement could terminate as early as age 18, this is not the preferred way to leave funds to a grandchild who cannot handle money. A trust or annuity might be a better choice.

One little quirk associated with custodial accounts is that the balance would be included in the custodian's taxable estate. If you have a taxable estate ($1.5 million in 2004 and 2005), it might be better not to serve as custodian, particularly if you are in poor health. Your estate could get stuck with paying federal estate taxes on the account balance, even though it all would go to the child upon attaining the age of majority!

Custodian of a Will. Someone having custody of a deceased person's will is a fiduciary in a limited sense. State laws often require the custodian of an original will to file it with the probate court within a specified period of time after learning of the person's demise. The will must be filed with the court even if all assets were jointly owned and even if there will not be a probate. The purpose of the filing requirement is to make the will a matter of public record.

INDEX

ABOUT THE AUTHOR

JON A. IVERSON has practiced law for more than 30 years, principally in the areas discussed in this book. His wide range of experience is reflected in the clarity with which the topics are discussed. He is a member of the National Associaion of Elder Law Attorneys.